1989

A BYRON CHRONOLOGY

A Byron Chronology

NORMAN PAGE

G.K.HALL&CO.

70 LINCOLN STREET, BOSTON, MASS.

Published 1988 in the United States of America and Canada by
G. K. HALL & CO.
70 Lincoln Street
Boston, Massachusetts 02111

First published 1988 by
THE MACMILLAN PRESS LTD
Houndmills, Basingstoke
Hampshire RG21 2XS

Printed in Hong Kong

Library of Congress Cataloging-in-Publication Data
Page, Norman.
A Byron chronology.
Bibliography: p.
Includes index.
1. Byron, George Gordon Byron, Baron,
1788–1824—Chronology.   I. Title.
PR4387.P34   1988   821′.7   87–24776
ISBN 0–8161–8952–8

Contents

List of Maps

General Editor's Preface

Most biographies are ill adapted to serve as works of reference – not surprisingly so, since the biographer is likely to regard his function as the devising of a continuous and readable narrative, with excursions into interpretation and speculation, rather than a bald recital of facts. There are times, however, when anyone reading for business or pleasure needs to check a point quickly or to obtain a rapid overview of part of an author's life or career; and at such moments turning over the pages of a biography can be a time-consuming and frustrating occupation. The present series of volumes aims at providing a means whereby the chronological facts of an author's life and career, rather than needing to be prised out of the narrative in which they are (if they appear at all) securely embedded, can be seen at a glance. Moreover, whereas biographies are often, and quite understandably, vague over matters of fact (since it makes for tediousness to be forever enumerating details of dates and places), a chronology can be precise whenever it is possible to be precise.

Thanks to the survival, sometimes in very large quantities, of letters, diaries, notebooks and other documents, as well as to thoroughly researched biographies and bibliographies, this material now exists in abundance for many major authors. In the case of, for example, Dickens, we can often ascertain what he was doing in each month and week, and almost on each day, of his prodigiously active working life; and the student of, say, *David Copperfield* is likely to find it fascinating as well as useful to know just when Dickens was at work on each part of that novel, what other literary enterprises he was engaged in at the same time, whom he was meeting, what places he was visiting, and what were the relevant circumstances of his personal and professional life. Such a chronology is not, of course, a substitute for a biography; but its arrangement, in combination with its index, makes it a much more convenient tool for this kind of purpose; and it may be acceptable as a form of 'alternative' biography, with its own distinctive advantages as well as its obvious limitations.

Since information relating to an author's early years is usually scanty and chronologically imprecise, the opening section of some volumes in this series groups together the years of childhood and adolescence. Thereafter each year, and usually each month, is dealt with separately. Information not readily assignable to a specific month or day is given as a general note under the relevant year or month. The first entry for each month carries an indication of the day of the week, so that when necessary this can be readily calculated for other dates. Each volume also contains a bibliography of the principal sources of information. In the chronology itself, the sources of many of the more specific items, including quotations, are identified, in order that the reader who wishes to do so may consult the original contexts.

NORMAN PAGE

Introduction

Interest in Byron's biography began during his lifetime, accelerated rapidly almost as soon as the news of his death reached England, and has remained at a fairly consistently high level ever since. There is, consequently, a multitude of items, ranging from multi-volume books to articles in periodicals, dealing not only with Byron himself but with almost every significant member of his circle; and to this we must add letters, diaries and other material not originally intended for publication but sometimes offering exact and useful information or illuminating insights. Much, perhaps most, of this attention, however, has concerned itself less with the patient disentangling of facts necessary in order to get the record straight than with the grinding of adulatory or hostile axes, and with the dramatic re-creation of, and sometimes sensational speculation concerning, his emotional and sexual life. The present volume has the more modest, and more sedate, objective of presenting a record of Byron's life as it was lived from year to year, and confines itself to such facts as can be ascertained with reasonable precision and confidence. At the same time, the genuine drama of Byron's life and career, and the complexity and fascination of his personality, give even a chronological record its own narrative interest; and the method provides some striking juxtapositions – of Byron's public and private doings, for instance, and of the conduct of his various relationships and the connection between his social and personal life and the composition of his poems. For those who prefer or need to use the book simply as a work of reference, its arrangement and index should make the checking of a single point or an enquiry into a particular topic relatively painless.

In common with any compilation of its kind, this *Byron Chronology* reflects the availability of sources, which at various points can range from the over-abundant to the non-existent, and sometimes suffers from their absence. A consistent degree of coverage is in the nature of things impossible to achieve: there are periods, especially in the early years, for which we would certainly like to know more, and plenitude of material is sometimes the result of accident rather than an indication of exceptional importance. Nevertheless, a clear if not complete picture of Byron's extraordinary and unprecedented career does seem to emerge. Unsurprisingly, Byron's own letters and journals have been the major source of detailed information; happily for an enterprise such as this, Byron was, unlike some writers, reasonably conscientious in dating his letters and not often demonstrably careless in his references to dates and periods of time. It would clearly be foolish, however, to allow Byron's to be the only 'voice' to be heard, vigorous and engaging though it usually is; and additional dimensions have been given to the record by incorporating the voices and verdicts, transmitted through their own letters, journals and reminiscences, of some of those who were close to him at various stages of his life – both those, such as Shelley and Scott, who are noteworthy in their own right, and those who would otherwise be forgotten – and whose viewpoints enable us to see him from the outside.

In my *Byron: Interviews and Recollections* I have suggested and exemplified the unreliability of some of the published accounts, such as those of Medwin and Trelawny. This chronology, which concentrates on the known facts as a basis for biographical and critical enquiry, may help to serve as a corrective or counterbalance to the wilfully prejudiced and self-indulgently fictionalised versions of the truth that have long been current, and not always estimated at their true value.

Throughout this volume, 'tells' usually signifies that the information or opinion is communicated in a letter. Where Byron's letters are quoted from, their date is the date of the entry unless otherwise noted. A few major contemporary events have been included, but no attempt has been made to duplicate the valuable services performed by such compilations as Neville Williams' *Chronology of the Modern World* (1966).

List of Abbreviations

Throughout this chronology B signifies Byron, who is to be taken to be the subject of all verbs for which no subject is indicated. *I&R* refers to *Byron: Interviews and Recollections*, ed. Norman Page (1985). Titles of Byron's works are abbreviated as follows:

AB	*The Age of Bronze*
BA	*The Bride of Abydos*
CH	*Childe Harold's Pilgrimage*
DJ	*Don Juan*
EBSR	*English Bards and Scotch Reviewers*
FP	*Fugitive Pieces*
H&E	*Heaven and Earth: A Mystery*
HI	*Hours of Idleness*
L&J	*Byron's Letters and Journals*, ed. Leslie A. Marchand (see Select Bibliography).
MF	*Marino Faliero*
PC	*The Prisoner of Chillon*
Sard	*Sardanapalus*
SC	*The Siege of Corinth*
TF	*The Two Foscari*
VJ	*A Vision of Judgement*

Map 1   Byron's travels, 1809–11

BYRON'S TRAVELS
1809 – 1811

BLACK SEA

TURKEY

ITALY

ALBANIA

Constantinople

SEA OF MARMORA

Tepelene

Abydos

Jannina

Troy

Corfu

Tenedos

GREECE

Lesbos

Prevesa

ÆGEAN SEA

Smyrna

Thebes

Ephesus

Ionian Islands

Kea

Patras

Athens

Tripolitza

Corinth

Girgenti

SICILY

Valetta

Malta

SEA

Crete

(Reproduced from Leslie A. Marchand, *Byron: A Portrait* (London: John Murray, 1971) pp. 64–5)

Map 2   Byron's Greece

Samothrace

Mount Athos

Sestos
•Abydas

Hellespont
(Dardanelles)

Plains of
Troy

MITYLENE
OR LESBOS

ÆGEAN

ΒΟΕΑ

CHIOS

Smyrna

.Marathon

SEA

E.
A
hens

olonni
nium)

Kea

Paros
Antiparos

NAXOS

(Reproduced from Leslie A. Marchand, *Byron: A Portrait* (London: John Murray, 1971) pp. 410–11)

A Byron Chronology

Early Years (1788–1804)

1788 (22 Jan) George Gordon Byron* is born in lodgings at 16 Holles Street, Cavendish Square, London, only child of John Byron (1756–91) and his second wife, Catherine, *née* Gordon (1765–1811), who had married on 13 May 1785 at St Michael's Church, Bath. John Byron, the eldest son of the second son of the fourth Lord Byron, had previously married (in 1779) Amelia, Lady Carmarthen (died 28 Jan 1784), the divorced wife of the Marquess of Carmarthen, who had borne him a daughter, Augusta Mary (born 26 Jan 1784), half-sister of B. In the autumn of 1787, B's parents had gone to France to escape their creditors, but had returned separately to England not long before his birth. The child is born with a clubbed right foot and is seen by John Hunter, the famous surgeon. (29 Jan) B is christened at Marylebone parish church.

1789 (14 July) Storming of the Bastille. During this summer, Mrs Byron and her son leave London for Aberdeen and settle in lodgings in Queen Street, where she lives on £150 a year; in August they are joined by Captain Byron, but before long he returns to the Continent.

1791 (2 Aug) Death of John Byron at Valenciennes, France, possibly by suicide. Soon afterwards Mrs Byron moves to 64 Broad Street, Aberdeen.

* On B's pronunciation of his own surname, Moore's letter of 9 February 1831 to an American enquirer, W. M. Robinson, provides the following information: 'Your letter, which had been delayed some time at Mr Murray's, has just reached me. I fear you will not find the decision of your wager a very easy matter, as Lord Byron, at different periods of his life, pronounced his name differently, and therefore may be said to have adopted both the modes of pronunciation to which I take for granted you allude. During all the first part of my acquaintance with him he called himself Bȳron, with the y long, but it was, I believe, at the time of his marriage, that he changed it to Bўron, with a short y, and in this manner I rather think he pronounced his name ever after – though, singularly enough, he taught some of his Italian friends, to whom this latter mode would have been so much more convenient, to call him according to his first manner of pronunciation Bȳron.'

At the age of four or five, B spends a year at John Bowers' school in Long Acre, Aberdeen.

1794 As a result of the death of William Byron, grandson of the fifth Lord Byron, at the siege of Calvi in Corsica, B becomes heir to the peerage.

1794–8 B attends Aberdeen Grammar School. During these early years he reads widely; later he tells John Murray that by the time he was eight he had read the Old Testament 'through and through'. In 1795 his portrait is painted by John Kaye of Edinburgh. At about this time he meets his cousin, Mary Duff, and falls in love with her.

1798 (21 May) Death of William, fifth Lord Byron, grand-uncle of B, who now inherits the title. In August, B and his mother leave Aberdeen for Newstead Abbey, Nottinghamshire, family seat of the Byrons, and live there for a few months. B is made a ward in Chancery and Lord Carlisle becomes his guardian. B meets the Clarke family of Annesley Hall, including Mary Chaworth, a distant cousin (see 1803). His earliest surviving letter is written from Newstead on 8 November.

1799 Mrs Byron settles in Nottingham and B is sent to a tutor to be prepared for entrance to a public school, returning to Newstead during the holidays. He lodges with the Parkyns family in Nottingham and the daughters of the house fall in love with him. He is attended by May Gray, his nurse, who is later dismissed after B reveals that she has been for a considerable time in the habit of entering his bed for sexual purposes, and also of beating him when drunk (see also 1 Sep). He is seen by a quack-doctor, Lavender, who attempts unsuccessfully to improve the condition of his foot. In July he is taken to London by John Hanson, arriving on the 12th. On 1 September Hanson writes to Mrs Byron that B has complained to him of May Gray's behaviour: 'He told me that she was perpetually beating him, and that his bones sometimes ached from it; that she brought all sorts of Company of the very lowest Description into his apartments; that she was out late at nights, and he was frequently left to put himself to bed. . . .' In September B becomes a pupil at Dr Glennie's school in Dulwich, where he remains until Easter 1801. (Glennie later recalls that B showed 'an intimate acquaintance with the historical parts of the Holy Scriptures'.) He spends Christmas with the Hanson family at Earl's Court.

1800 B continues at Dr Glennie's. He spends the summer holidays with his mother in Nottingham and Newstead; falls in love with his cousin Margaret Parker; and makes his 'first dash into poetry'.

1801 In April Hanson takes B to Harrow to meet Dr Joseph Drury, headmaster of Harrow School, who later records his impression during this first interview that 'a wild mountain colt had been submitted to my management'. B becomes a pupil at Harrow; his tutor is Dr Drury's son, Henry Drury, and among his contemporaries is Robert Peel. Another contemporary, Edward Noel Long, describes B in a letter home on 1 May as 'a lame fellow . . . he seems a good sort of fellow'. The summer holidays are divided between London and Cheltenham; in London he stays with his mother in lodgings at Mrs Massingberd's, 16 Piccadilly, and with the Hansons in Earl's Court. The Christmas holidays are spent with his mother.

1802 B continues at Harrow. He spends the Christmas holidays at Bath with his mother, and attends a masquerade dressed as a Turkish boy.

1803 (19 Jan) Mrs Byron writes to Hanson that her son '*positively refuses*' to return to Harrow as a pupil of Henry Drury; he does, however, return there in the following month. (4 Feb) Dr Drury writes to Hanson that the reason for B's desire for a change of tutor is 'the repeated complaints of Mr Henry Drury respecting his inattention to business, and his propensity to make others laugh and disregard their employments as much as himself'. (1 May) B writes to his mother that Mr Drury 'has behaved himself to me in a manner I neither *can* nor *will bear*' (after B had been talking to a fellow-pupil in church, Drury did not reprimand him but, taking the other boy aside, called B a blackguard). (26 July) B leaves Harrow for Southwell, Nottinghamshire, where his mother has rented Burbage Manor. After spending a few days with her, he moves to the lodge at Newstead, home of the steward, Owen Mealey; he makes frequent visits to Annesley Hall and falls 'distractedly in love' (Mrs Byron's phrase) with Mary Chaworth; later in life he tells Medwin that Mary was 'the *beau idéal* of all that my youthful fancy could paint of beautiful'. In September he refuses to return to Harrow. In November he moves into Newstead Abbey as the guest of Lord Grey de Ruthyn, who in March 1803 has leased it, and remains there until January 1804. During this year he becomes friendly with the Earl of Clare, a Harrow pupil four years younger than himself. According to his later statement (to Moore, 22 Aug 1813), B first encounters Moore's poetry at about this time.

1804 (22 Jan) B's sixteenth birthday. At the end of January, after breaking off his friendship with Lord Grey – apparently because the latter made sexual advances to him – B returns to Harrow; later he describes Grey as 'that object of my cordial, deliberate detestation' (to Augusta Byron, 2 Nov 1804). By 22 March he is back at Burgage Manor for the Easter holidays, but returns to Harrow in April. In late July he again leaves Harrow for Burgage Manor. He has formed a friendship with Elizabeth Pigot, daughter of Southwell neighbours, and during this summer he sees a good deal of the Pigots and also visits Annesley Hall to see Mary Chaworth, who is soon to be married. (See 'The Dream'.) He also hears that Mary Duff is married, and is much affected by the news. In September he returns to Harrow. In November Mrs Byron urges him to effect a reconciliation with Lord Grey, but he refuses. (2 Dec) Napoleon is crowned Emperor in Paris. (5 Dec) Harrow term ends; on Dr Drury's advice, B leaves the school with the intention of not returning but of working under a private tutor for his entrance to a university; in the event he changes his mind and returns to Harrow in the following February. During the Christmas holidays he remains in London at the home of the Hansons; he goes to Covent Garden Theatre and sees the celebrated boy actor, the 'Young Roscius' (William Betty).

1805

(22 Jan) B's seventeenth birthday. In February he returns to Harrow. At Easter, Dr Drury retires as headmaster and is succeeded by Dr George Butler; B has recently described Drury as 'the best master we ever had' (to Augusta, 2 Nov 1804) and has

said, 'What little I have learnt I owe to him alone' (to Augusta, 17 Nov 1804); and Francis Hodgson later reports that B used to speak of Drury as 'the *dear* Drury, in contradistinction to his successor, whom he maliciously designated the *cheap* Butler, but whom he afterwards learned to estimate at his proper value' (see also Feb 1808).

April

3   (Wed) B leaves Harrow and goes to the Hansons.
4   Tells Augusta that he is in very low spirits.
7   Leaves for Burgage Manor to visit his mother, with whom he quarrels.
30 (approx.) Arrives back in London.

May

8   (Wed) Harrow terms begins; B is soon in trouble for leading a rebellion against the new headmaster.

June

6   (Thurs) Speech Day at Harrow; B recites a speech from Young's *The Revenge* (see also Sep 1808).

July

1   (Mon) B visits Cambridge and is entered (i.e. admitted as a member, though he does not go into residence) at Trinity College.
4   Second Harrow Speech Day; B recites a speech from *King Lear*.

August

2   (Fri) B plays in the Eton–Harrow cricket match and scores 18 runs; Harrow are beaten. Afterwards the teams dine together, drink a good deal of wine, go to London, visit the Haymarket Theatre, and are involved in rowdy behaviour; the next morning B cannot remember how he got to bed. This marks the end of B's schooldays; much later (1821) he declares, 'I always *hated* Harrow till the last year and a half, but then I liked it.' Before leaving the school he carves his name on the school-room wall.
3   Sets off for Southwell.
4   Arrives at Burgage Manor. During this visit his relationship

with his mother deteriorates further: on 18 August he tells Augusta, 'The more I see of her the more my dislike augments.'

September

23 (Mon) Leaves Southwell for London, where he stays with the Hansons.

October

21 (Mon) Battle of Trafalgar.

24 Goes into residence at Trinity College, Cambridge. His rooms are in the south-east corner of Great Court; the keeping of dogs being forbidden, B later (see 26 Oct 1807) keeps a tame bear in a turret at the top of the staircase. During his time at Cambridge, he becomes romantically attached to John Edleston, a choirboy at Trinity College chapel.

November

6 (Wed) Tells Augusta that he likes college life 'extremely'.

December

18 (Wed) Goes to London and spends the Christmas vacation in lodgings as Mrs Massingberd's, 16 Piccadilly, remaining there until April 1806.

27 Tells Augusta that he has been extravagant, is short of money (his allowance is £500 a year, with a servant and a horse), and proposes to borrow 'a few Hundreds' from money-lenders. Augusta, whom he asks to act as a guarantor for this debt (since he is under age), offers to lend him money, but he declines (7 Jan 1806) and Mrs Massingberd and her daughter act instead.

1806

January

22 (Wed) Byron's eighteenth birthday.

February

5 (Wed) Cambridge term begins, but B remains in London, where he frequents the theatres and the fencing establishment

at 13 Bond Street of Henry Angelo, and plunges into dissipation.
26 Tells his mother that he is entertaining the idea of spending 'a couple of Years' abroad and that he does not intend to return to Cambridge; he also tells her that he has paid his '*Harrow* Debts' and his college bills, but admits to being 'naturally extravagant'.

March
10 (Mon) Tells Hanson that he needs to raise £500 to pay his debts.

April
In the middle of the month B leaves London and returns to Cambridge, remaining there until about 12 July; he then returns to London and soon afterwards proceeds to Southwell, where he again quarrels with his mother. By this time he is preparing a volume of poems (*Fugitive Pieces*) to be printed by John Ridge of Newark.

August
7   (Thurs) Returns to London.
10 Sends some 'Stanza's', written that evening, to John Pigot (probably the poem 'To Mary') for including in FP. (When he departed from Southwell in a hurry, his poems had been left with Ridge, and the proofs seem to have been sent to the Pigots.)
18 Goes to Worthing, Sussex, then visits his Harrow and Cambridge friend Edward Noel Long in Littlehampton, Sussex. In the following month, he returns to Southwell, and soon afterwards makes an excursion to Harrogate, Yorkshire, with John Pigot. Back in Southwell again, he stays with the Pigots and is involved in private theatricals, playing parts in two plays, Cumberland's *Wheel of Fortune* and Allingham's *Weathercock*.

October
9   (Thurs) Writes 'To Miss E[lizabeth] P[igot]'.
28 Writes 'Granta, A Medley'.

November

During this month *FP* is privately printed.

7 (Fri) Writes 'To M. . . .', addressed to Anne Houson.
15 Writes the lines 'To Miss H[ouson] . . .'.
23 Writes 'The First Kiss of Love'.

December

1 (Mon) Writes 'To a Knot of Ungenerous Critics'.
29 Writes 'The Prayer of Nature'.

1807

January

Early in the month *Poems on Various Occasions* is privately printed. A presentation copy is sent to Dr T. Talkner (Mrs Byron's landlord) on the 8th and one to John Pigot on the 13th.

13 (Tues) Tells John Pigot that he is in love with Anne Houson.
22 B's nineteenth birthday.
30 Has a discussion with Captain John Leacroft, brother of Julia Leacroft, whom B has been courting; discovering that the Leacrofts have taken his intentions seriously, B writes to Captain Leacroft the next day to say that he will avoid social contacts with the family in future.

February

6 (Fri) Tells the Earl of Clare that, among other activities, he has been 'making *love*' and 'taking physic' – the latter perhaps being the first reference to his dieting (see 2 Apr below).
14 Tells the Revd Thomas Jones that he never wished to go to Cambridge and was 'originally intended for Oxford'. (On 19 November 1820 he tells Murray that he could not go to Oxford because there were no vacant rooms at Christ Church.)
25 Writes the poem 'Egotism'.

March

6 (Fri) Tells William Bankes that he has 'a large volume [of poems] in Manuscript' – i.e., *Hours of Idleness* – but lacks the time and inclination to prepare it for publication; later in the month, however, he tells Bankes that he is preparing the volume 'for the Public at large' (unlike his previous two

volumes, which had been privately printed), and that it will appear in the latter part of May.

8   Writes 'To the Author of a Sonnet . . .'.
15 Writes 'To an Oak in the Garden of Newstead Abbey . . .'.

April

2   (Thurs) Tells John Hanson that he is dieting 'by violent exercise, & Fasting', and has lost 18 pounds since January. Two weeks later he tells Edward Noel Long that he has lost 23 pounds, having reduced a weight of 14 stones 6 pounds (202 pounds) to 12 stones 11 pounds (179 pounds). Later in the month he is down by another 9 pounds, and on 14 May he tells Long that he is now down to 12 stones (168 pounds), and intends to reduce further to 11 stones (154 pounds). At the end of June he is still reducing and is 'barely 11 stone' in his clothes; by 13 July he is 'below 11 stone considerably' and still getting thinner; by 20 August he is 10 stone 11 (151 pounds), and by 13 January 1808 his weight is 10½ stones (147 pounds).

16 In a revealing letter to Long, B states that he is a Deist and regards himself as 'destined never to be happy' and as 'an isolated Being on the Earth'.

19 Writes to Hanson concerning his financial difficulties.

June

Hours of Idleness published by Ridge of Newark.

27 (Sat) B arrives in Cambridge on a short visit to settle his affairs, and sees John Edleston again.

July

4   (Sat) Spends the evening with Edleston – a farewell meeting, since Edleston is going to London in October to begin a business career. The next day he tells Elizabeth Pigot that he loves Edleston 'more than any human being', and that he is 'the only *being* I *esteem*'.

5   Tells Elizabeth Pigot that he has decided to spend another year in residence at Cambridge (i.e. the academic year 1807–8).

6   Goes to London, staying at Gordon's Hotel, Albemarle Street.

13 Reports himself to Elizabeth Pigot as 'in a perpetual vortex of dissipation'.

21   Sends to Ben Crosby, publisher of *Monthly Literary Recreations*
      and London agent for the distribution of *HI*, a review of
      Wordsworth's 1807 *Poems*; the review is published soon
      afterwards. On the same day, he sends Crosby 'Stanzas to
      Jessy', also published (anonymously) in the July issue of the
      Monthly. The same issue contains a favourable review of *HI*.

August

 2   (Sun) Tells Elizabeth Pigot that he has written 380 lines of a
      blank verse poem 'Bosworth Field' and plans to extend it to
      eight or ten books and to finish it within a year (it was never
      finished and the manuscript has not survived). By the 11th
      he has finished the first book and started the second, and is
      expecting the project to occupy three or four years.
Early in the month he swims three miles in the Thames, from
Lambeth and under Westminster and Blackfriars bridges.
11   Tells Elizabeth Pigot that he is about to set off for Scotland,
      the Hebrides and Iceland; he will collect material for a book of
      translations from the Erse. The tour is, however, cancelled,
      perhaps for financial reasons.
During the summer he makes several trips into the provinces.

October

19   (Mon) Asks Hanson to send his quarter's allowance since he
      is down to 'one *solitary Guinea, two bad sixpences* and a *shilling*'.
26   Back in Cambridge by this date, and finds it 'a villainous
      Chaos of Dice and Drunkenness' (to Elizabeth Pigot). On the
      25th and 26th he is up until 4 a.m. playing at Hazard. He tells
      her that in January he intends to go to sea for several months
      with his cousin, Captain George Bettesworth – another plan
      that fails to materialise. He also tells her that he has acquired
      a tame bear; that he has been 'praised to the Skies' in the
      Critical Review for September and 'abused' in *The Satirist* for
      October; and that he has written 214 pages of a novel, a
      poem of 380 lines (an early version of *EBSR*), 560 lines of
      'Bosworth Field', 200 lines of another poem, and various
      short poems.

November

11   (Wed) Writes to Ridge concerning a second edition of *HI*,

published in the following year under the title *Poems Original and Translated*.

During this month the *Eclectic Review* publishes a review of *HI*.

December

22 (Tues) Refers to a review of *HI* that has appeared in the *Monthly Review*. By this date he has agreed to contribute a poem of over 400 lines to a volume of verse that will also contain J. C. Hobhouse's imitation of Juvenal's eleventh satire; in the event, B contributes nine poems to *Imitations and Translations* (1809).

After Christmas he leaves Cambridge for good.

1808

January

6 (Wed) By this date B is in London, staying at Dorant's Hotel in Albemarle Street.

12 In a letter he refers to the December issue of the *Antijacobin Review and Magazine*, which has published a favourable review of *HI*.

20 Tells R. C. Dallas that he is regarded by some as 'the votary of Licentiousness, and the Disciple of Infidelity'; on the next day, in another letter to Dallas, he refers to himself as 'the *wicked* George L[or]d B[yron]'.

22 Byron's twentieth birthday.

24 Dallas sees Byron, and dines with him on the 27th.

25 Tells Hanson that his debts amount to over £5000 (see 18 Nov).

February

2 (Tues) Tells James de Bathe that in the spring of 1809, soon after he comes of age, he will set off on a voyage to the Eastern Mediterranean (see 7 Oct).

Early in the month he visits Harrow and is reconciled to Dr Butler; on the 11th he instructs Ridge to omit the poem 'Childish Recollections', which refers satirically to Butler, from the second edition of *HI*.

25 Attends a masquerade; his supper-companions are 'seven whores, a *Bawd* and a *Ballet-master*' (to Hobhouse, 27 Feb).

The next day he tells the Revd John Becher that he is 'nearly worn out' by sexual activity with his sixteen-year-old mistress Caroline (not identified). Towards the end of this month, the January issue of the *Edinburgh Review* appears, containing an unfavourable review by Henry Brougham of *HI*.

March
Early in the month B falls ill as a result of his dissipation; on the 14th he tells Hobhouse that he has been confined to his room for five days. At about this time William Fletcher becomes his valet and serves him until B's death.

28 (Mon) By this date B has seen a copy of *Poems Original and Translated*, published during this month.

April
During this month, with the assistance of John ('Gentleman') Jackson, the famous pugilist and former champion, B organises a fight between Tom Belcher and Dan Dogherty.

15 (Fri) Tells Hobhouse that he and his friends have 'kept it up, with the most laudable systematic profligacy'. At this time B is keeping two mistresses as well as amusing himself with the French mistress of an artist and 'occasionally an Opera Girl'.

May
10 (Tues) B goes to Hertfordshire to watch a prize-fight.

June
16 (Thurs) Goes to Brighton.

July
Visits Cambridge early in the month and takes his MA degree (on the 4th); later he returns to Brighton and spends several more weeks there with a party of friends that includes Hobhouse and Davies.

August
Continues in Brighton.

September
After Lord Grey has moved out of Newstead Abbey, B takes up residence there with Hobhouse as a companion. By the middle of

the month he is organising private theatricals – a performance of Young's *The Revenge* is which Hobhouse and other friends participate.

October
7   (Fri) Tells his mother that she is not welcome at Newstead at the present time, and that he plans to visit Persia the following spring.

November
1   (Tues) At about this time B and Hobhouse dine at Annesley Hall, and B sits next to Mary Chaworth (see the poems 'Well! Thou art happy' and 'To a Lady on Being Asked my Reason for Quitting England in the Spring').
2   Tells his mother that he will go to India next March; the intention is repeated to Hanson on the 18th.
10   B's Newfoundland dog, Boatswain, goes mad and dies; on the 20th he writes the poem 'Inscription on the Monument of a Newfoundland Dog'.
18   Tells Hanson that his debts amount to about £12,000; that he will never sell Newstead Abbey, but will pass it on to his heir; and that by spending six months on a voyage to India he will actually save money.
30   Repeats (this time to Augusta) that he will not sell Newstead Abbey. Hobhouse leaves Newstead before the end of the month.

In the later months of this year B is working again on *EBSR*.

1809

Early in the year B's friend Edward Noel Long is drowned at sea. Work on *EBSR* continues in the first three months of the year.

January
15   (Sun) Tells Hanson that he will take his seat in the House of Lords as soon as possible (see 13 Mar).
22   B's twenty-first birthday, celebrated at Newstead with an ox-roasting and other traditional festivities – in B's absence, for by the 19th he is installed at Reddish's Hotel in St James's

Street, London, where Dallas calls on him on this date by invitation and finds him 'in high spirits; indeed, so high as to seem to me more flippant on the subject of religion, and on some others, than he had ever appeared before'. One of the servants left behind at Newstead to take care of the house is Lucy, a maid whom B has made pregnant; she later bears him a child (see 'To my Son').

Towards the end of this month, B offers *EBSR*, through Dallas, to Longman's, who refuse it, then to Cawthorne, who accepts it.

February

8 (Wed) Tells Hanson that his creditors are so pressing that, if he does not have money, he must go abroad; he repeats that he will not sell Newstead Abbey.

21 Goes to the opera (King's Theatre): see lines 608–31 of *EBSR*.

March

6 (Mon) Tells his mother that he is depressed by the death (in a duel) of his friend Lord Falkland. Later he gives financial assistance to Falkland's widow and stands godfather to his posthumous child.

13 Takes his seat in the House of Lords: for an account, see Dallas excerpted in *I&R*, pp. 8–10 (Dallas has called at his hotel by chance and been invited to accompany him to the House).

Shortly afterwards, *EBSR* is published.

April

By the early part of this month B is back at Newstead, and the famous party takes place with the guests attired as monks. At this time Hanson tries, on B's orders, to obtain a mortgage on Newstead Abbey, but is unsuccessful.

16 (Sun) Tells Hanson that he has 'no alternative' but to leave England, and has booked his passage for 6 May. His letter hints obscurely at 'circumstances' that have not been identified.

25 Back in London and installed at Batt's Hotel, Jermyn Street. Soon afterwards B works on the revisions for the second edition of *EBSR*.

May

The second edition of *EBSR* appears about the middle of the month. At about the same time B sends his protégé Robert Rushton back to Newstead after discovering that Fletcher has not only visited prostitutes himself but has taken the boy to one (see 6 June).

June

6 (Tues) B sends instructions that Rushton, who has evidently been forgiven, should join him in London.

19 Accompanied by Hobhouse, B leaves London for Falmouth, where he stays at Wynn's Hotel. Fletcher, whom B had resolved to dismiss, has pleaded successfully and is still in B's service; he, Rushton, and an old servant named Joe Murray will accompany B on his voyage (see 16 Aug).

July

2 (Sun) After a long wait for a favourable wind, B and Hobhouse sail for Lisbon on the packet *Princess Elizabeth.*

7 They arrive in Lisbon, where B swims across the Tagus and he and Hobhouse engage in sight-seeing and attend the theatres.

12–16 They visit Cintra.

17 They set off to ride to Cadiz, covering some seventy miles a day (according to B's letter to Hodgson, 6 Aug).

25 They arrive in Seville and spend three days there; they have difficulty in finding lodgings and on the night of arrival go 'supperless and dinnerless to bed' (Hobhouse's diary).

29 They arrive in Cadiz, and the next day attend a bull-fight.

August

3 (Thurs) They sail on the frigate *Hyperion* from Cadiz, past Cape Trafalgar, to Gibraltar, where they stay from the 4th to the 16th.

7 Sir Walter Scott writes to Robert Southey, 'it is funny enough to see a whelp of a young Lord Byron abusing me [in *EBSR*], of whose circumstances he knows nothing, for endeavouring to scratch out a living with my pen'.

15 B meets John Galt.

16   After sending all his servants except Fletcher back to England,
     B sails to Malta with Hobhouse on the packet *Townshend*; Galt
     is among their fellow passengers.
26   They spend the evening with Galt.
27   They arrive in Cagliari, Sardinia, where B dines and goes to
     the theatre with Galt and others.
31   They arrive in Malta after calling at Girgenti, Sicily. On
     arrival in Malta, according to Galt's account, all the passengers
     go ashore except B and Hobhouse, who remain behind in the
     expectation of 'a salute from the batteries'; when nothing
     happens, they disembark, are unable to find lodgings, and
     turn up at the home of Mr Chabot, a merchant, where Galt
     and others are sitting over their wine after dinner, to beg 'a
     bed and morsel for the night'.

September
In Malta, B falls in love with Mrs Constance Spencer Smith and
(18th) challenges Captain Cary, aide-de-camp to General Oakes,
to a duel (Drury offers an apology and the duel does not take
place).
 9   (Sat) B and Hobhouse dine with General Oakes, 'who had
     been next to Nelson when he lost his eye' (Hobhouse); Mrs
     Spencer Smith is present. Hobhouse notes in his diary that B
     'is, of course, very popular with all the ladies, as he is very
     handsome, amusing, and generous'.
16   'In case your thoughts are still the same as they were on the
     16th of September, 1809, then set out for Malta on the very
     first opportunity' (Mrs Spencer Smith, letter of Nov 1810).
21   B and Hobhouse sail for Greece and Albania on the brig
     Spider.
23   They obtain their 'first sight of Ancient Greece from the
     Channel betwixt Cephalonia and Zante' (Hobhouse).
26   They land at Patras, then proceed to Prevesa in Albania,
     arriving there on the 28th.
29   They visit the ruins of Nicopolis.

October
 1   (Sun) They set off for Jannina, a three-day journey through
     mountainous country, arriving on the 5th.
11   They set off for Tepelene, spending a night at the monastery
     at Zitsa *en route* (the 12th).

19   They arrive in Tepelene, where B visits Ali Pasha, 'who made
     some observations on the smallness of Lord Byron's ears, by
     which he averred . . . that he could discover him to be of an
     ancient house' (Hobhouse).
22   'Byron is all this time engaged in writing a long poem in the
     Spenserian stanza' (Hobhouse); but see 31st.
23   They leave Tepelene to return to Jannina, arriving there on
     the 26th.
31   According to his own statement, B begins *Childe Harold's
     Pilgrimage.*

November
3   (Fri) They leave Jannina, and are back in Prevesa by the 8th.
10   While travelling in a Turkish ship near Corfu, they narrowly
     escape shipwreck in a storm.
11   B attends a Greek wedding.
12   B tells Hanson that he intends to spend a year in Greece
     before proceeding to Asia, and that he will never return to
     England if he can avoid it.
13   They leave Prevesa for Patras and Athens. On the 20th they
     are at Missolonghi, and they arrive in Patras on the 22nd.

December
4   (Mon) They set off for Athens.
5   At Vostitza.
7   They have a glimpse of Mount Parnassus covered with snow.
14   They cross the Gulf of Corinth and arrive in Salona at
     midnight.
15   Visit Delphi.
19   At Sudavia.
22   Visit Thebes.
25   Arrive in Athens, where they spend ten weeks.
30   B finishes the first canto of *CH* and begins the second almost
     immediately (see 3 Jan 1810).

1810

January
1   (Mon) Thomas Moore writes to B asking if he may 'consider your
     Lordship as the author of [*EBSR*]', in which lines 458–61 refer

facetiously to Moore's duel with Jeffrey (see also 22 Oct 1811 and 28 Nov 1818).
3   B is writing the twelfth stanza of canto II of *CH*.
22   B's twenty-second birthday.
23   B and Hobhouse visit Sunium and Marathon.

February
Towards the end of the month B is writing the stanzas on Albania in canto II of *CH*.
21   (Wed) B meets Galt again, and they see each other from time to time until B's departure from Athens.
28   B, Hobhouse and Galt visit the Parthenon.

March
5   (Mon) B and Hobhouse set sail on the *Pylades* for Smyrna.
8   They arrive in Smyrna; while there, B sees Galt again.
13   They visit Ephesus.
19   B tells his mother that he has 'traversed the greater part of Greece' and is now *en route* for Constantinople; once there, he will decide whether to extend his travels into Persia or to return. His entourage now consists of Fletcher, two Albanian soldiers, and a Greek interpreter, Andreas Zantachi.
28   Finishes the first draft of canto II of *CH* (revised and slightly enlarged in the early part of 1811).

April
11   (Wed) They set sail for Constantinople on the 36-gun frigate *Salsette*.
15   They visit the Troad and see the site of Troy while the *Salsette* is at anchor for a fortnight.

May
3   (Thurs) At the second attempt, B swims from Sestos to Abydos with Lieutenant Ekenhead while the *Salsette* is in the Dardanelles awaiting a favourable wind (see 'Written after Swimming from Sestos to Abydos', dated 9 May, and *DJ*, II. 105).
5   Tells Hodgson that he is 'tolerably sick of vice' (cf. 28 June).
13   The *Salsette* anchors at Constantinople; B and Hobhouse go ashore the next day.
15   B and Hobhouse call on Stratford Canning, British diplomat.

21 They visit the bazaars and the seraglio.
28 'So far we have dined every night with the Ambassador' (Hobhouse); but on this day B is offended when Canning refuses to walk behind him in an official procession, and it takes him 'quite three days to get over this trivial contretemps' (Hobhouse).

Towards the end of the month B quarrels with Fletcher and determines to send him back to England, but relents after Fletcher pleads to be allowed to remain. The same resolution is taken again, and again rescinded, a few weeks later.

June
7 (Thurs) B writes 'Farewell Petition to J. C. H[obhouse] Esq.'.
Around the middle of the month, they make an expedition through the Bosphorus to the Black Sea.
28 B tells his mother that he has 'laid down a resolution to reform, and *lately* kept it'.
30 B tells Hanson that he does not intend to return to England for at least two years.

July
10 (Tues) At the invitation of the British Ambassador, Robert Adair, B attends his final audience with the Sultan, Mahmoud II.
14 B and Hobhouse leave Constantinople on the *Salsette*.
17 They arrive at Zea (Keos); Hobhouse, who has acccompanied B throughout his year's travels, now bids him farewell 'on a little stone terrace at the end of the bay, dividing with him a little nosegay of flowers', and returns to England.
18 B arrives in Athens – 'a place which I think I prefer upon the whole to any I have seen' (to his mother, 20 July) – and is greeted by Lord Sligo.
19 Receives visits from Frederick North, Henry Knight and John Fazakerly, three English travellers in Greece.
21 Leaves Athens for the Morea; Lord Sligo accompanies him as far as Corinth, where they separate, B proceeding to Patras.
25 At Vostitza, B finds Eustathius Georgiou, a Greek boy whom he had probably met there the previous year, and who now joins his entourage.
26 Arrives at Patras and is entertained by the British consul, Strané.

28 Quarrels with Eustathius, but they are reconciled; within a couple of weeks, however, B sends him home.

August

Early in the month B is at Tripolitza, where he visits Velly Pasha, who presents him with a stallion. Soon after the middle of the month, he sets off for Argos, where he meets Lord Sligo again, and before the 23rd (perhaps by the 19th) he is once more back in Athens, staying at a Capuchin monastery at the foot of the Acropolis and already planning another tour of Attica.

23 (Thurs) Tells Hobhouse that he rides to the Piraeus every day and swims for an hour.

September

12 (Wed) Lady Hester Stanhope arrives in Athens; B meets her several times.

In the latter half of this month, B, accompanied by his young protégé Nicolo Giraud and two Albanian servants, makes another tour of the Morea; on or about the 22nd he falls ill with fever at Patras, is confined to bed for five days, and reports himself to Hobhouse on the 25th as 'much debilitated'. During this tour he visits Olympia.

October

2   (Tues) Still at Patras.

13 Returns to Athens, and again stays at the Capuchin monastery.

November

11 (Sun) Tells Hanson that, in spite of serious financial difficulties, he still refuses to sell Newstead Abbey, as Hanson has urged him to do.

28 Sandford Graham, a Trinity contemporary, dines with B.

December

During this month B makes a second visit to Sunium.

1811

January

B continues in Athens.

14 (Mon) B sends Fletcher back to England. He writes to his mother, 'I have done with authorship'.

18 Tells Hanson that he needs more money but is still determined not to sell Newstead.

20 Tells Francis Hodgson that he is studying modern Greek.

22 B's twenty-third birthday.

February

1 (Fri) Tells Hanson that he intends to visit Jerusalem and Cairo.

March

2–18 Still in Athens, B writes the first draft of *Hints from Horace*, and during the next few months copies it, with corrections, twice. (See also 28 Mar 1820.)

5 (Tues) Tells Hobhouse that he frequently attends dinners and balls given by the English colony in Athens.

The Curse of Minerva (dated 17 Mar) is also written during this month.

April

22 (Mon) Accompanied by Nicolo Giraud, B sets sail on the *Hydra*, arriving in Malta on the 30th.

May

B spends this month in Malta.

15 (Wed) Tells Hobhouse that he is suffering from a severe attack of fever; later (7 July) he tells Henry Drury that while at Malta he was treated by Tucker, an army surgeon, for 'a *Gonorrhea*, a *Tertian fever*, & the *Hemorrhoides*'.

16 Writes the facetious verses 'Epitaph for Mr Joseph Blackett, Late Poet and Shoemaker'.

22 Writes a memorandum to himself listing seven reasons for being weary of life.

June

2 (Sun) Leaves Malta on the frigate *Volage*, accompanied by two

Greek servants, Demetrius Zograffo and Spiro Saraci. Nicolo Giraud remains in Malta.

July

14 (Sun) Lands at Sheerness, Kent, after an absence from England of two years and twelve days. He proceeds to London, where he again stays at Reddish's Hotel, St James's Street.

15 Dallas visits B and later reports: 'I thought his looks belied the report he had given me of his bodily health, and his countenance did not betoken melancholy, or displeasure at his return. He was very animated in the account of his travels, but assured me he had never had the least idea of writing them. He said he believed satire to be his *forte*, and to that he had adhered . . . .'

17 Meets Hobhouse by arrangement at Sittingbourne, Kent; they spend the next two days in visiting Canterbury and neighbourhood.

Shortly afterwards, B submits the manuscript of the first two cantos of *CH* to the bookseller William Miller, who by the 30th has declined to publish it. By the end of the month, Dallas, acting on B's instructions, has offered the manuscript to John Murray, who agrees to publish it. At the end of the month B hears of the death of his friend John Wingfield.

August

1 (Thurs) Death of B's mother: 'I heard *one* day of her illness, the *next* of her death' (to John Pigot, 2 Aug). B leaves at once for Newstead on hearing the news, spends the night of the 2nd at Newport Pagnell, and arrives on the 3rd.

7 B hears that his Trinity friend Charles Skinner Matthews has drowned while bathing in the Cam on 3 August. He tells Davies that he is 'almost desolate': 'My mother lies a corpse in this house, my best friend is drowned in a ditch'.

12 B drafts a new will, which, among other bequests, leaves £7000 to Nicolo Giraud.

About the middle of the month, Scrope Davies visits B, who finds his company 'very reviving' but feels 'solitary and sullen' after Davies's departure for Harrogate (to Hobhouse, 30 Aug).

21 Tells Augusta that he will go abroad again as soon as he has set his affairs in order.

September

14 (Sat) B tells Murray of his annoyance that the manuscript of
CH has been shown to William Gifford, editor of the *Quarterly
Review*. At about this time, B receives a visit from John
Claridge, a Harrow school-fellow, whom B finds dull.

October

?5 (Sat) Accompanied by Hanson, B sets out for Rochdale,
Lancashire, where he owns coal-mines.

9 Back at Newstead. Very soon after his return, he hears that
John Edleston has died in May; on the 13th, he tells
Hobhouse, 'I have been more affected than I should care to
own elsewhere'; on the 28th he tells Mrs Pigot that he has
suffered six bereavements within four months.

11 Writes 'Epistle to a Friend . . .'.

16 Goes to Cambridge to visit Davies.

22 Moore writes to B, referring to his earlier letter (see 1 Jan
1810), and stating that, although his 'injured feeling still
remains', his changed circumstances (he has recently married)
prevent him from pursuing the matter – in other words, he
has dropped the idea of a challenge. B replies on the 27th,
stating that he never received the earlier letter, and his reply
reassures Moore ('you had no intention of charging me with
falsehood . . . the objectionable passage of your work was
not levelled personally against me').

28 B arrives in London, where he stays at 8 St James's Street.
During the visit he sees Dallas and other friends.

November

4 (Mon) Dines with Samuel Rogers and meets Moore for the
first time; Thomas Campbell is also present. After dinner they
discuss the merits of Walter Scott and Joanna Baillie. The
occasion is described, not without malice, in *Recollections of the
Table Talk of Samuel Rogers*, excerpted in *I&R*, p. 18.

Towards the end of the month B visits Cambridge again, and is
back in London by 3 December.

December

9 (Mon) Sees Rowe's *Fair Penitent*, with Robert Coates (a
wealthy amateur actor known as 'Romeo Coates') as Lothario,
at the Haymarket Theatre.

11   Invites Moore to accompany him to Newstead.
16   Dines with Rogers; afterwards they attend one of Coleridge's lectures.
19   Accompanied by Hodgson and Harness, B leaves London for Newstead, where he falls in love with a Welsh maid, Susan Vaughan (see 28 Jan 1812).

1812

January
 4   (Sat) Still at Newstead Abbey, B tells Hanson that his creditors are 'extremely pressing'.
11   Goes to London (8 St James's Street), and is embroiled in legal business.
20   Attends another of Coleridge's lectures, again with Rogers.
22   B's twenty-fourth birthday.
28   Breaks off his relationship with Susan Vaughan, who has written to him reproachfully.
31   Attends the House of Lords but does not speak; he catches a cold there and is unwell the next day.
During this month B reviews W. R Spencer's *Poems* for the *Monthly Review*.

February
Early in the month B is ill and in pain with '*Stone* in the *kidney*' (to Hobhouse, 10 Feb); he has recovered by the 10th but is on a strict diet and expects the affliction to be chronic. His creditors continue to be pressing, and he is arranging to sell the furniture and effects at Newstead Abbey.
16   (Sun) Tells Francis Hodgson that in the spring of 1813 he will leave England 'for ever' and settle in the eastern Mediterranean.
22   At a banquet held at Carlton House, the Prince Regent heaps violent abuse on the Whigs; when his daughter, Princess Charlotte, sheds tears at this outburst, she is ordered out of the room (see 7 Mar).
27   B delivers his maiden speech (on the Frame-breaking Bill) in the House of Lords; in a letter to Hodgson (5 Mar) B describes his manner as 'a sort of modest impudence' and his delivery as 'perhaps a little theatrical'. This is the first of three

speeches he makes there (see also 21 Apr 1812 and 1 June 1813).

March

2   (Mon) 'An Ode to the Framers of the Frame Bill' is published anonymously in the *Morning Chronicle*.

3   Cantos I and II of *CH* are published by Murray. B sends copies to Lord Holland, Samuel Rogers and others before publication. The edition is sold out within a few days, and Dallas later recalls that on the day of publication he found B 'loaded with letters from critics, poets, authors, and various pretenders to fame of different walks, all lavish of their raptures'. 'The triumphant success of [*CH*] in March 1812 marks the beginning of a new phase in Byron's relation with reviewers and public' (Andrew Rutherford). Moore later reports B as saying, 'I awoke one morning and found myself famous.'

7   'Sympathetic *Address* to a Young Lady' published anonymously in the *Morning Chronicle* (see 22 Feb for the incident that provoked the poem).

At about this time B meets Lady Caroline Lamb at Holland House.

25   Annabella Milbanke see B for the first time and records her impressions in her diary (see also 14 Apr).

April

2   (Thurs) At Lord Glenbervie's.

14   At Lady Cowper's, B talks to Annabella Milbanke; afterwards she writes to her mother that 'he wants that calm benevolence which could only touch my heart. He is very handsome, and his manners are in a superior degree such as one should attribute to Nature's gentleman.'

19   Writes 'To Samuel Rogers, Esq.'.

21   Speaks again in the House of Lords, this time on the Catholic Claims Bill; Hobhouse records in his diary that B 'kept the House in a roar of laughter'.

During this month B's relationship with Lady Caroline Lamb develops.

May

During this month the *Edinburgh Review* publishes (in its issue dated Feb) a favourable review of *CH* by its editor, Francis Jeffrey ('a volume of very considerable power, spirit and originality'). The poem is widely read and discussed: on 21 April Coleridge writes to his wife that 'All the world is talking of it'; Scott writes to friends about it on 4 April and 4 May; Wordsworth discusses it with Henry Crabb Robinson on 24 May; George Ellis reviews it in the *Quarterly Review* (issue dated Mar 1812).

1   (Fri) B tells Lady Caroline Lamb that he has been reading poems (in manuscript) by Annabella Milbanke and has been impressed by them.

7   At an evening party, B tells Mary Berry that he is 'very pleased' with Jeffrey's review of *CH* (see above).

18 Watches the execution at Newgate of John Bellingham, who has murdered Spencer Perceval in the House of Commons.

June

During this month the Evangelical journal the *British Review* publishes a favourable review of *CH*.

4   (Thurs) B sets off for Newstead with Hobhouse; they spend the night of the 4th at Market Harborough and reach Newstead on the 5th; by the 13th they are back in London.

Towards the end of June, B meets the Prince Regent 'at an evening party at Miss Johnson's', the Prince having 'expressed a desire to be introduced to him', and they have a long conversation 'on poetry and poets' (Murray to Scott, 27 June).

July

3   (Fri) 'Went to Byron, who agrees to go out of town' (Hobhouse). Scott writes to B and refers to the 'high pleasure' his poetry has given him; B replies on the 6th (the two do not meet until 1815).

8   'Byron went with me to my father's to-day at Whitton' (Hobhouse).

19 B dines with Hobhouse and Sinclair.

29 A planned elopement with Lady Caroline Lamb does not take place. Lady Melbourne, Lady Caroline's mother-in-law, subsequently asks B to leave London; soon afterwards he promises her that he will not see Lady Caroline and writes a farewell letter to her.

August

12 (Wed) Lady Caroline Lamb leaves her husband but does not join B; later B takes her back to her home.

14 Newstead Abbey is put up for auction but is not sold; on the 15th, Thomas Claughton offers £140,000 for it and the offer is accepted, but Claughton later has second thoughts and after more than two years of wrangling fails to complete the purchase.

23 By this date B is in Cheltenham.

September
During this month B begins *The Giaour*; he works on it for the rest of the year.

5 (Sat) Asks Murray what offer he will make for an additional six cantos of *CH*; he also asks Murray for copies of Scott's *Rokeby* and James MacKittrick's *Essay on Diet and Regimen*.

10 Tells Lord Holland that he has burned his unfinished draft of an address to be delivered on the opening night of the rebuilt Drury Lane Theatre (Holland has invited B to enter the competition announced by the theatre's Committee of Management). (See 23rd.)

14 Napoleon enters Moscow.

19 Tells Lady Melbourne that he could love Miss Milbanke 'if she would let me'.

23 Sends Lord Holland a draft of his Drury Lane Address (see 10th). He sends revisions in three letters on the 24th and numerous other letters during the next few days. (His entry is unsuccessful, but the decision is attacked by some of the newspapers; James and Horace Smith's famous volume of parodies, *Rejected Addresses* (1812), which B admires, is based on this competition and includes a parody of B's work.)

October
8 (Thurs) Annabella Milbanke writes a 'Character' of B.

10 B's 'Address' is delivered at the reopening of Drury Lane Theatre.

17 B tells Murray that he has 'in *hand* a *satire* on *Waltzing*' – i.e. 'The Waltz', published anonymously the following spring.

19 Napoleon's retreat from Moscow begins.

23 The *Morning Chronicle* publishes B's 'Parenthetical Address, by Dr Plagiary', a parody of one of the Drury Lane Addresses rejected by the Committee.

24 B leaves Cheltenham for Eywood, Lord Oxford's estate, and remains there until 21 November. During this period and

subsequently, Lady Caroline Lamb, who is in Ireland, sends him a number of letters, to which he replies coldly.
During this month B proposes to Miss Milbanke through Lady Melbourne, and is rejected in a letter from Miss Milbanke to Lady Melbourne on the 12th. He also visits Berkeley Castle and meets, among other guests, the famous clown Joseph Grimaldi.

November
4	(Wed) B tells Lady Melbourne that he likes the district very much and is arranging to occupy a house about five miles from Eywood the following year.
10	Tells Lady Melbourne that he has grown fatter in recent months.
21	Returns to Cheltenham; then stays briefly with Lord Jersey at Middleton; then proceeds to London, arriving on the 30th and staying at Batts' Hotel in Dover Street.
27	Tells Hobhouse that he is 'still remote from *marriage*'.

December
14	(Mon) By this date B is back at Eywood as Lord and Lady Oxford's guest, and remains there over Christmas.

1813

January
1–17	B is still at Eywood, pursuing his affair with Lady Oxford. During this period Lady Caroline Lamb continues to assail him with troublesome and even threatening letters; she also harasses him by forging a letter in his name to Murray, and stealing a portrait of him.
3	(Sun) Tells Hodgson that he is a 'great admirer' of James and Horace Smith's volume of parodies *Rejected Addresses*, and particularly likes the 'imitation' of *CH*; in a postscript he says that he has 'no intention' of continuing *CH*.
17	At Ledbury, *en route* for London.
19	Back in London, B settles in lodgings at 4 Bennet Street, St James's.
22	B's twenty-fifth birthday.
During this and the next month, B meets and corresponds with Caroline, Princess of Wales, to whom he has been introduced by Lady Oxford.

February

27 (Sat) Tells Hanson that he intends to go abroad again 'almost immediately'. The next day he refers again to an impending journey in a letter to Lady Melbourne.

Claughton's delay over completing the purchase of Newstead Abbey (see 14 Aug 1812) causes B much vexation at this time.

March

24 (Wed) Instructs Murray to undertake a private printing of fifteen copies of *The Giaour* (see 5 June). Tells Charles Hanson that at the end of May he will leave for Sardinia and the Levant.

25 B refers to the continuing problem of his debts.

26 Tells Augusta that he cannot 'afford to marry without a fortune'.

28 Returns to Eywood with the Oxfords.

April

 5 (Mon) Tells Lady Melbourne that he will open no further letters from Lady Caroline Lamb, and will hate her 'to the latest hour of my life'.

 7 Tells Lady Melbourne that, Lady Caroline having asked for a lock of his hair (perhaps as a condition of her returning the stolen picture: see 1–17 Jan), he has sent her instead a lock of Lady Oxford's.

24 B is back in London by this date.

29 Replies to a threatening letter from Lady Caroline and agrees to see her once more before he leaves England.

May

14 (Fri) Hears that Lady Oxford is ill (she has 'burst a small bloodvessel') and is blaming him for it; he suspects the report may be a fabrication. Lady Jane Davy writes to a correspondent that B is 'talking of Greece with the feelings of a poet and the intentions of a wanderer'.

16 Sends Murray a corrected proof of *The Giaour* incorporating an additional 160 lines or so. During the next few weeks he makes further revisions and additions.

20 Visits Leigh Hunt in prison and is introduced to him by Moore; B's visit is repeated a few days later.

26 Helen Stewart writes that B tells her he is going abroad soon.

During this month B visits Rogers and asks permission to dedicate *The Giaour* to him; he also meets Maria Edgeworth. Hobhouse's *Journey through Albania* is published.

June

1   (Tues) Speaks for the last time in the House of Lords.

?3   Leaves London for a few days with Lady Oxford; is back on the 8th and leaves again on the 9th to rejoin Lady Oxford at Portsmouth (she is on her way to Sardinia); returns to London later in the month. B now plans to leave England in July.

5   *The Giaour* published; B has already circulated privately printed copies to friends, but the published version is considerably longer as a result of the additions he has made during the past few weeks.

8   Thanks John Galt for his book *Letters from the Levant*, recently published and containing an account of his meeting with B in 1809.

20   Meets Madame de Staël (Lady Blessington later records B's opinion that the French writer was 'certainly the cleverest, though not the most agreeable woman he had ever known').

21   Catherine Fanshawe writes to a correspondent that 'Had the whole discourse [between B and Madame de Staël] been written, without one syllable of correction, it would be difficult to name a dialogue so full of eloquence and wit'.

22   Sends Murray some *'important'* revisions for the second edition of *The Giaour*.

27   Sees Madame de Staël again, at Lady Davy's, and introduces Augusta to her.

28   Lady Oxford leaves England; B is much affected by her departure.

July

Early in the month the second edition of *The Giaour* appears. The poem is favourably reviewed by Jeffrey in the *Edinburgh Review* dated July 1813.

5   (Mon) At about this time, B sees Lady Caroline Lamb again. Augusta is in London, and B is also seeing her.

12   Dines again with Madame de Staël. During this month, B's social life in London is very active, and by the 25th he

confesses to Moore that his brains are 'muddled' with excessive eating and drinking.

13 Tells Moore that he is attracted to Lady Adelaide Forbes and would marry her if his 'prospects' were better. He is anxious to go abroad, but is experiencing difficulty in obtaining 'a passage in a ship of war'.

28 Dines with Rogers and Richard Brinsley Sheridan.

August

1 (Sun) Leaves London for a week's visit to Augusta at Six Mile Bottom, near Newmarket. Augusta returns to London with him and plans to accompany him on his travels; the affair between them flourishes at this time. He turns down the offer of a passage on the *Boyne*, due to sail from Portsmouth early in the month, since places are available only for himself and a servant.

In the early part of the month he works on additions to *The Giaour* for the third edition; he sends 33 lines to Murray on the 10th, and on the 12th tells Webster that the length of the poem in the new edition will be 'nearly doubled'; by the 22nd it runs to over 1000 lines. Before this latter date, the third edition has appeared and B is busy with revisions for the fourth edition, containing 1048 lines, which appears before the end of the month (the first edition had contained only 684 lines).

6 Tells Henry Fox that he has been asked by Davies to act as a second in a gambling-quarrel with Lord Foley, but has played the role of peacemaker and the dispute has been settled.

22 Tells Moore that London is 'awfully empty', and that he has been discouraged from embarking on his travels by reports of plague and quarantine in the Mediterranean countries; he is now contemplating a visit to Russia.

Towards the end of the month he corresponds with Annabella Milbanke.

September

The fifth edition of *The Giaour* (1215 lines) appears early in the month (B tells Moore on the 1st that it is 'printing'), and the sixth towards the end of the month; eight further editions appear in 1814–15.

2 (Thurs) Tells Webster that in the Mediterranean countries he can live for half of the cost of residing in England; that Rogers

has invited him to accompany him on a visit to the Lake District; and that he 'almost' wishes he were married.

Towards the middle of the month, B leaves London on another visit to Augusta. He is back in London by the early morning of the 15th after spending a night with Davies in Cambridge, and carousing with him, on the way back. Later in the month he visits Webster at Aston Hall, Rotherham, Yorkshire: he is there by about the 17th, and on his way home (at Stilton, Huntingdonshire) on the 25th, having left (as he tells Annabella on the 26th) to escape the Doncaster races.

26 Visits Holland House and meets Southey.

30 Dines at Holland House, the Queen also being among the guests. He meets John Curran, Irish judge, there, and finds him 'quite fascinating' (to Moore, 1 Oct).

October

5 (Tues) By this date B is back with the Websters in Yorkshire and pursuing a 'Platonic' affair with Webster's wife, Lady Frances (he writes a long account of the affair to Lady Melbourne on 8 and 10 Oct).

10 Visits Newstead Abbey, accompanied by Webster. Tells Hanson that he wishes to lend £1000 to Webster.

11 B and Webster return to Aston.

13 Tells Lady Melbourne that he is 'totally absorbed' in his affair with Lady Frances, and is ready to elope with her if necessary.

16 Back at Newstead Abbey, with the Websters as his guests, by this date.

17 After over-indulgence in wine the previous night, B is unwell. At about this time he has an opportunity to seduce Lady Frances but declines to do so after she has told him she would not be able to 'bear the reflection' afterwards.

19 Tells Lady Melbourne that he has 'thrown away the best opportunity that ever was wasted upon a spoiled child'.

19 At Northampton, on his way back to London, accompanied by Webster.

20 Back in London. Webster leaves the next day.

November

1 (Mon) Begins *The Bride of Abydos*. A first draft is finished by the 8th, and by the 11th B has completed a fair copy which is sent immediately to Murray. On the 12th he begins correcting

proofs; on the same day he asks Gifford, who has already read the poem in manuscript, to look at a proof; and he makes revisions and additions over the next two weeks.

14 Begins to keep a journal, continued until 19 April 1814.

15 Goes to see *Antony and Cleopatra* ('a salad of Shakespeare and Dryden': *Journal*) at Covent Garden.

17 Presents to Murray a portrait of himself by Thomas Phillips.

22 Sends a list of those who are to receive presentation copies of *BA* to Murray; the list includes Gifford, Lord Holland, Lady Melbourne, Hodgson and Lady Caroline Lamb.

23 Dines with J. W. Ward; George Canning is also present.

24 Dines with a party of pugilists, including 'Gentleman' Jackson, and their fans.

27 The plague still placing difficulties in the way of Mediterranean travel, B is planning to visit Holland, and perhaps to go into Germany and Italy, with J. W. Ward.

December

1 (Wed) Tells Hodgson that Murray has offered him 1000 guineas for *Giaour* and *Bride*; he has declined receiving payment of the sum for six months, by which time Murray will know whether the success of the poems enables him to afford it.

2 *BA* published; four more editions appear before the end of the year, and five more in 1814. B tells Hunt that he would like their friendship to be 'permanent'.

3 Thanks Zachary Macaulay, editor of the *Christian Observer*, for a review of *The Giaour* (probably by J. W. Cunningham) that has appeared in that periodical. Sees Galt for the last time; Galt's later recollections of the meeting include the statement that B 'explained to me a variety of tribulations in his affairs, and I urged him, in consequence, to marry, with the frankness which his confidence encouraged'.

8 Dines at Holland House and sees Madame de Staël again: she and B are 'very good friends' (*Journal*). Tells Moore that 'not a day passes' when he does not think and speak of him.

10 Dines with Rogers and Richard Sharp. B has fasted for the previous forty-eight hours (he is dieting dramatically at this time), and wishes he 'could leave off eating altogether' (*Journal*).

13 Has been reading some of Burns's unpublished letters, lent to

him by Dr John Allen, a member of the Holland House set, and finds them 'full of oaths and obscene songs' (*Journal*).

15   Leaves London for a few days.
17–18   Writes two sonnets addressed to Lady Frances Webster ('To Genevra').
18   Begins *The Corsair*. Canto II is begun four days later.
27   Begins to make a fair copy of *The Corsair*; the task is completed within four or five days.
28   Dallas calls on B.

1814

January
16 or 17   Finishes correcting proofs of *The Corsair*.
16   (Sun) 'A wife would be my salvation' (*Journal*).
17   Leaves London with Augusta to spend 'a few days' at Newstead; in the event he is away for almost three weeks, thanks to bad weather.
22   B's twenty-sixth birthday.

February
During this month B's 'Sympathetic Address to a Young Lady' (see 7 Mar 1812), also known as 'Lines to a Lady Weeping', which has been republished at the end of *The Corsair*, causes him to be bitterly attacked by the Tory press.

 1   (Tues) *The Corsair* published; it sells 10,000 copies on the day of publication – 'a thing perfectly unprecedented' (Murray to B, 3 Feb).
 6   Leaves Newstead for London; in the course of the journey he writes letters from Newark.
 9   Reaches London in the evening.
10   Goes to Covent Garden; Hobhouse joins him in his private box.
19   Sees Edmund Kean in *Richard III*.
20   Reads Schiller's tragedy *The Robbers*.
28   Moore tells B that a rumour has been circulating in London that B has made him a present of the proceeds of *The Corsair*; during this month Moore also reminds him that B has appointed him his 'Editor & Historiographer'.

During this month B sees Hobhouse again, the latter having returned from an eight-month Continental tour on 8 February.

March

1 (Tues) Dines with Rogers; among those also present is Sheridan.

10 Goes to Covent Garden with Hobhouse to see Sheridan's *The Trip to Scarborough*.

11 Hobhouse notes in his diary that he 'gave dinner to Lord Byron at the Cocoa-Tree [a fashionable club in St James's Street] in payment of a bet respecting allies reaching Paris by the twenty-third of last month'.

14 Dines with Rogers.

17 Practises sparring with Jackson; notes in his journal that he is in good physical condition and that his arms are very long for his height of 5 feet 8½ inches. Reads Isaac D'Israeli's *Quarrels of Authors*, recently published.

19 Spars with Jackson again. 'Dined at the Cocoa-Tree with Byron on fish alone' (Hobhouse); afterwards they sit together in B's rooms in Bennet Street until 1 a.m.

20 Reads Machiavelli and other authors; also the latest number of the *Edinburgh Review*, which pays him a 'high compliment' (in a review of Maria Edgeworth's *Patronage* he is described as 'the first poet of his time').

21 Attends a party at Lady Lansdowne's and introduces Hobhouse to Lady Melbourne.

22 Attends a party at Lady Charlotte Greville's, and afterwards notes in his journal that such occasions are a 'deplorable waste of time'.

23 With Hobhouse, calls on Lady Portsmouth and Lady Westmoreland.

27 Dines with Davies; between them they consume six bottles of claret and one of champagne.

28 Spars with Jackson again. Moves into 2 Albany, which he has taken on a seven-year-lease.

April

B is away from London for six days at the beginning of the month, returning to London on the 7th. During this period he visits Six Mile Bottom with Augusta. His 'Ode to Napoleon Buonaparte' is written during this month and is referred to in the

Morning Chronicle on the 21st. (By the Treaty of Fontainebleau, signed on 11 Apr, Napoleon abdicates and is banished to Elba; B's journal entries for the 8th and 9th refer to the situation in France.)

8   (Fri) Practises sparring with Jackson; he tells Moore the following day that he has been doing so daily for the past month as well as drinking and eating heavily.

11   Hobhouse calls on B, who agrees to go to Paris with him (but changes his mind the next day, leading Hobhouse to note in his diary that he 'is a difficult person to live with'.

Towards the middle of the month, B is busy preparing a new edition of *The Corsair*.

19   The journal begun on 14 November 1813 is discontinued and is subsequently given to Moore, who is told to keep it (letter of 14 June).

May

4   (Wed) Attends a party at Lady Jersey's, and another at Lady Cahir's the next day (typical of numerous similar social engagements during this period).

7   Attends a performance of *Othello*, in which Kean plays Iago, at Drury Lane, and afterwards describes Kean's acting as 'perfection'.

9   Hobhouse calls on B; Moore calls while they are together.

14   Begins *Lara*.

19   B, Hobhouse and Moore go to see Kean in *Othello*; afterwards they meet Kean.

June

14   (Tues) Tells Moore that he thinks of leaving London and going to Newstead soon. Attends a supper at Lady Rancliffe's. *Lara* is finished by this date (published on 6 Aug).

23   Attends a party at Lady Jersey's.

24   Writes to Murray concerning the proofs of *Lara*.

26   Dines at Lord Cowper's.

27   Thanks Rogers for the manuscript of his poem *Jacqueline*, subsequently published in the same volume as *Lara*. Sends Murray some additions to *Lara*. In the evening, at Lord Sussex's.

July

1   (Fri) Dressed as a monk, B attends a masked ball at Burlington House held in honour of the Duke of Wellington.

3   Leaves London for a short visit to Six Mile Bottom.
6   Dines with Hobhouse and Davies in Cambridge.
7   Returns to London, setting off from Cambridge at 2 p.m. by coach with Hobhouse, Davies and Kinnaird; all four dine at the Cocoa-Tree.
8   Asks Hodgson to rent a house for him in Hastings, where he intends to spend a short period with Augusta and her children. (Hodgson rents Hastings House on B's behalf.)
20 Leaves London for Hastings.
24 In a letter to Murray, B gives high praise to Scott's *Waverley*, recently published.
During this month Jeffrey's review of *Corsair* and *BA* appears in the *Edinburgh Review* (issue dated Apr 1814).

August
3   (Wed) The sale of Newstead Abbey to Claughton has fallen through, and Claughton has agreed to forfeit £25,000 of his down-payment. B writes to Moore that the affair has ruined him and that he intends to settle at Newstead.
10 Tells Annabella, with whom he is corresponding at this time, that he loves her.
11 Back in London for a short period.
17 Sees Claughton, who is still pursuing the question of his purchase of Newstead Abbey.
20 Leaves London for a visit to Newstead with Augusta and her children.

September
9   (Fri) Sends another proposal – this time directly, but somewhat obscurely worded – to Annabella Milbanke.
15 Tells Moore that, if a 'circumstance of importance' (i.e., his proposal) does not come to fruition, he will go to Italy. But on the 18th he receives a favourable response from Miss Milbanke, and an invitation from her father to visit them at Seaham, near Durham; plans for leaving England are abandoned, and he replies immediately, telling her that after a visit to London on business he will proceed to Seaham. On the same day he tells Hanson that he is engaged, and raises with him the question of marriage settlements.
21 Goes to London.
26 B's skull is examined by Johann Spurzheim, the German

phrenologist, who finds all the characteristics 'strongly marked' but 'very antithetical', so that his 'good & evil are at perpetual war' (B to Miss Milbanke).

October

5 (Wed) Writes to the editor of the *Morning Chronicle* to protest at a contradiction published in that paper of the announcement in a Durham paper of B's forthcoming marriage.

7 Tells Lady Melbourne that his solicitor, Hanson, is ready to meet Sir Ralph Milbanke's and will propose a settlement of £60,000 (i.e. to produce an income of £300 a year). B still desires to sell Newstead as a way of raising capital. He tells Moore that he is 'in the road to matrimony', and that his fiancée, whom he has not seen for ten months, is 'perfection'.

14 Dines with Kean and others.

15 Sends a present of game to Leigh Hunt, who is still in prison (see 20 May 1813; Hunt is released on 2 Feb 1815).

19 Hobhouse receives a letter from B inviting him to 'stand groomsman at his marriage'.

20 Tells Annabella that he is writing *Hebrew Melodies*.

24 Complains to Hanson that he is unduly delaying the completion of the legal arrangements in preparation for his marriage.

29 Leaves London and spends the night and most of the next day at Six Mile Bottom.

31 In Newark, having spent the night of the 30th at Wansford.

November

2 (Wed) Arrives in Seaham.

4 Tells Lady Melbourne that he dislikes his future mother-in-law, and that Annabella is 'the most *silent* woman I ever encountered – which perplexes me extremely'.

16 Leaves Seaham for London; spends the night at Boroughbridge, Yorkshire.

17 Arrives at Newstead.

18 Spends the night at Cambridge (Sun Inn), where he sees Hodgson.

19 Goes to visit Augusta at Six Mile Bottom, remaining there until the 22nd.

22–3 In Cambridge again, to vote for his friend William Clark, who is competing for a medical chair.

24   Arrives in London.
26   Sees Kean in *Macbeth*.
28   In a letter to Annabella, gives high praise to Southey's poem *Roderick*, recently published.

December
16   (Fri) Writes to the Archbishop of Canterbury to request a special licence to marry Annabella Milbanke.
22   Visits Doctors' Commons, and receives the licence on the next day.
24   Accompanied by Hobhouse, B leaves London for Seaham.
25   At Six Mile Bottom.
30   Arrives at Seaham at 8 p.m. According to Hobhouse, 'Miss Milbanke is rather dowdy-looking . . . though she has excellent feet and ankles. Of my friend she seemed dotingly fond, gazing with delight on his bold and animated face. . . . Byron appears to love her personally, when in her company . . . .'
31   The marriage settlements are signed.
During this month, John Keats composes a sonnet 'To Lord Byron'.

1815

January
2   (Mon) B is married to Annabella Milbanke at 10 a.m. in the drawing-room at Seaham. According to Hobhouse, Annabella is 'as firm as a rock' during the ceremony; when B comes to the words in the marriage service 'With all my worldly goods I thee endow', he looks at Hobhouse 'with a half-smile'. The couple. then proceed to Halnaby, near Darlington, for the honeymoon (until 21st).
7   B tells Lady Melbourne that he has 'great hopes' that his marriage will turn out well – adding, however, 'but Time does wonders'.
21   B and his wife go to Seaham to pay a visit (unenthusiastically on B's part) to her parents, remaining there until 9 March.
22   B's twenty-seventh birthday.
27   Lady Milbanke, B's mother-in-law, tells a correspondent that the couple are 'both well, and as happy as youth and love can make them'.

February

2 (Thurs) B writes to Moore, asking him to send the latest London gossip (B is evidently finding life in his in-laws' house tedious).

10 Tells Moore that he has 'a plan of travel into Italy'. The intention is referred to again in a letter to Moore on the 22nd.

March

1 (Wed) Napoleon lands in France; he enters Paris on the 20th.

2 B tells Moore that he is in 'a state of sameness and stagnation'.

9 The Byrons leave Seaham and proceed to Six Mile Bottom, where they arrive on the 12th and stay with Augusta: a letter to Hanson on the 9th refers to a visit of 'a day or two', but in the event they remain until the 28th. While there, B hears of Napoleon's return.

27 Writes to Moore concerning the death of his daughter Olivia, B's god-daughter.

28 The Byrons proceed to London.

29 They settle at 13 Piccadilly Terrace. Hobhouse calls on them, and B advises him ' "not to marry", though he has the best of wives' (Hobhouse).

31 Tells Coleridge that he will help to find a publisher for his poems (Murray publishes the volume in the following year); he also urges him to write a tragedy and expresses regret for his satirical reference to Coleridge in *EBSR*.

April

4 (Tues) Hobhouse meets B and his wife at dinner at Sir Francis Burdett's: 'Lord Byron tells me he and she have begun a little snubbing on money matters. Marry not, says he.'

7 B meets Scott (they are introduced by Murray at his office), and they talk 'for nearly two hours' (Murray's diary). They meet again the next day, and frequently thereafter until B's departure from England. (For Scott's recollections of their first meeting, see Moore's *Life of Byron*, excerpted in *I&R*, pp. 38–9.) Augusta arrives for a visit that lasts more than ten weeks.

17 Death of Lord Wentworth, uncle of Lady Byron; B's mother-in-law inherits a substantial fortune, which is entailed upon Annabella and her children, and the Milbankes subsequently take the name of Noel.

29 Tells Hodgson that Lady Byron is 'in the Family Way'.
Hebrew Melodies is published during this month.

May
During the month, Augusta's stay with the Byrons in London continues. B joins the sub-committee of management of Drury Lane Theatre.

June
16 (Fri) B tells Hanson to make haste in drawing up his will. The will, which makes provision for Augusta and her children, is eventually signed on 29 July.
18 Battle of Waterloo.
20 George Ticknor, an American visitor armed with a letter of introduction from Gifford, calls on B and pays several other visits during the next few days.
27 Ticknor joins the Byrons and the Milbankes at Drury Lane, where Kean is acting.

August
30 (Wed) B leaves London to visit Augusta at Six Mile Bottom, she having returned there towards the end of June.

September
4 (Mon) Tells Webster that he is 'writing nothing'.
6 Scott, who is in Paris, writes to Joanna Baillie that he will 'endeavour to see you and Lord Byron or both in passing through London'.
14 B joins Scott and other friends for an early dinner; Scott later writes that he 'never saw Byron so full of fun, frolic, wit, and whim; he was as playful as a kitten' (he and B never meet again).

October
18 (Wed) Writes to Coleridge about the latter's poem *Christabel*, part of which has been repeated to him by Scott a few months earlier.
22 Writes to Hunt, praising his *The Story of Rimini*.
27 Thanks Coleridge for sending him a copy of *Christabel*, and urges him to complete it; he also sends Coleridge a portion of *The Siege of Corinth*, which he has been working on during

this month (B is evidently anxious to protect himself against a possible accusation of plagiarism).

30   Thanks Hunt for his *The Feast of the Poets*, which B praises. He tells Hunt that he disagrees with him about Wordsworth, whose promise B regards as 'unfulfilled'. Dines with a large party that includes Sheridan and Kinnaird.

November
 4   (Sat) Writes to Murray, recommending publication of *Christabel* and *The Story of Rimini* (see Oct); Murray publishes both in the following year.
15   Augusta arrives in London to stay with the Byrons.
25   Hobhouse writes in his diary that he called on B and adds, 'In that quarter things do not go well. Strong advice against marriage. Talking of going abroad.'

During this month B's creditors become pressing and bailiffs move into his London house.

December
10   (Sun) Birth of B's daughter Ada. On the 29th he tells Lady Holland that both mother and child are doing well.

1816

January
 2   (Tues) B returns to Murray a draft for 1000 guineas sent in payment for the copyrights of *SC* and *Parisina*; he tells Murray that, while he cannot accept the payment, he is willing to allow the poems to be published in his collected works; he will not, however, permit their separate publication as they are 'not . . . at all equal' to his 'notions of what they should be'. Murray nevertheless issues them in a separate volume five weeks later. B is heavily in debt at this time, and is making arrangements to give up his London establishment.
?10   Sends £21 to Hunt as a contribution to a charitable fund.
15   Lady Byron and the child leave London to join her parents at Kirkby Mallory, Leicestershire (she never lives with B again).
18   Lady Byron prepares a statement for her legal adviser.
20   B tells Rogers that he is willing for the payment he has declined from Murray (see 2 Jan) to be shared between

William Godwin (£600), Coleridge and Charles Maturin.
Murray demurs at this arrangement, and on the 22nd B asks
for the return of the manuscripts of the two poems, insisting
that 'they shall not be published at all'. (The project to assist
Godwin and the others does not materialise.)

22   B's twenty-eighth birthday.
23   Tells Rogers that he is unwell.

February

2   (Fri) Receives a letter from his father-in-law asking him to
     agree to a separation. Sir Ralph Noel's letter refers to the
     'treatment' Lady Byron has received from B and her 'dismissal'
     from his house. B replies at once that she was not dismissed
     but that they parted in 'real harmony', and that she left
     London on medical advice; the reply also refers to his financial
     straits and poor health. B refuses to commit himself on the
     question of separation. The next day he writes to his wife to
     ask her feelings on the subject and to tell her that he will
     abide by her decision and has nothing to blame her for.
     Having received no reply, he writes to her again on the 5th.

5   Hobhouse calls on B and finds him 'exceedingly depressed,
     more so than in an intimacy of eleven years he had ever
     seen'.

7   *SC* and *Parisina* published by Murray. B reads a letter from
     his wife addressed to Augusta and writes to his father-in-law
     to express his distress at its attitude towards himself; he
     states his willingness to welcome her back, or to join her, if
     she so desires. The same or the next day he receives a letter
     from Lady Byron addressed to himself and communicating
     her decision not to resume their life together.

8   Tells Hobhouse that he means to go abroad. Replies
     reproachfully but affectionately to his wife, tells her that she
     is 'much changed' in the three weeks since she left him, and
     asks to see her again.

13   Lady Byron tells B that she left his house because she believed
     he was in danger of becoming insane.

15   Asks his wife what 'charges' are being brought against him
     and refers to the rumours that are circulating concerning their
     separation; he ends the letter by declaring his continuing love
     for her. He writes to her again on the 21st and 28th, in the
     second of these letters asking for a reconciliation.

17   Henry Crabb Robinson reads aloud *SC* at an evening party in London and finds it (according to his diary) 'disgusting and horrid in its effects'.

March
During this month Newstead Abbey is shaken by a mild earthquake.
1   (Fri) Asks Lady Byron to grant him an interview, and repeats the request in another letter on the 4th.
4   In a second letter written to his wife on this day, he recognises that 'all hope is over' but reaffirms his love for her.
7–9   A mediator, Robert Wilmot, makes separate visits to B and his wife in an attempt to make arrangements for the separation.
9   'Lord Byron called in his carriage and took us to Drury Lane' (Hobhouse); they see Kean.
11   B writes to his wife in colder terms concerning legal and financial arrangements.
18   Writes the first draft of 'Fare Thee Well', and a few days later sends the poem to Lady Byron.
23   Tells Lady Holland that he hopes to leave England in the second week in April.
25–6   Writes three letters to his wife defending himself against the accusation of blaming her for what has happened or speaking of her unkindly; he asks Lord Holland and other friends to provide written testimony to this effect, and forwards their statements to her.
28   Engages John William Polidori as his travelling physician. Hobhouse calls on B.

April
At about this time B meets Claire Clairmont and their liaison begins.
3   (Thurs) Hunt, Davies and Hobhouse dine with B, Hobhouse having arrived at 13 Piccadilly Terrace for a visit to B.
5–6   Auction sale of B's library.
14   Tells Lady Byron that they 'can never meet again in this world – nor in the next', and that he has just said goodbye to Augusta, who is leaving London to return to Six Mile Bottom.
18   Wordsworth writes to a correspondent that B's talents are 'of a *mean* order'.

21 B signs a deed of separation.

22 Asks Augusta not to mention Lady Byron to him but to keep him informed concerning Ada's welfare. 'Rogers came to take leave of Byron. . . . Everything prepared for Byron's departure. All his papers put into my hands' (Hobhouse).

23 Leaves London and proceeds to Dover, B travelling with Davies in B's 'new Napoleonic carriage built by Baxter for £500' (Hobhouse); Polidori and Hobhouse travel down in a chaise. They arrive in Dover at 8.30 after an eleven-hour journey, and dine at the Ship. The *Morning Chronicle* this day announces B's departure from England. Property belonging to B and his servants and remaining at Piccadilly Terrace is seized by his creditors.

24 In the evening B and his friends visit the tomb of Charles Churchill in the graveyard at Dover: 'Byron lay down on the grave and gave [the old sexton] a crown to fresh turf it' (Hobhouse).

25 'Up at eight, breakfasted; all on board except the company. The Captain said he could not wait, and Byron could not get up a moment sooner. . . . However, after some bustle out came Byron, and, taking my arm, walked down to the quay. . . . He got on board a little after nine; the bustle kept Byron in spirits, but he looked affected when the packet glided off' (Hobhouse). Hobhouse waves him farewell as B sails to Ostend, *en route* for Geneva. His party includes Fletcher, Rushton, Dr Polidori and a Swiss guide (Berger), and his travelling-coach goes with him.

27 In Bruges.

28 In Ghent.

30 In Antwerp.

May

1–6 In Brussels, where they are detained for repairs to the carriage after three breakdowns. On the 4th (Sat) B visits the battlefield at Waterloo. The third canto of *CH* is begun at this time (on the 4th Polidori writes in his diary that B 'has written twenty-six st[anzas] to-day – some on Waterloo'). On the 6th the party sets off for Louvain.

8 In Cologne.

10–16 They travel up the Rhine via Bonn, Koblenz and Mannheim; on the 11th Polidori writes to Hobhouse that B's health is 'greatly improved' and his spirits 'much improved'. On the 16th B writes to Hobhouse from Karlsruhe. He intends to leave there on the 17th, but remains an extra day on account of Polidori's illness.

20   In Basle.

23   Travelling from Berne to Morat, B and Polidori 'had debates whether clouds were mountains, or mountains clouds' (Polidori's diary).

25   They arrive in Sécheron, near Geneva. In the register of the Hotel Angleterre, B puts down his age as 100.

27   B meets Shelley, who has arrived in Sécheron with Mary Godwin and Claire Clairmont on the 18th.

June

1   (Sat) The Shelleys move into Maison Chappuis, Montalegre, about two miles from Geneva. B visits them; according to Polidori, the subjects of after-dinner conversation include Rogers, whom B regards as a 'good poet' but 'malicious'.

2   B dines with Shelley again and afterwards goes on the lake with him and others.

4   Goes on the lake with Shelley and Polidori; B and Polidori quarrel.

10   B moves into the Villa Diodati (just above the Maison Chappuis), where Milton had stayed in 1639.

13   B and his boatman Maurice are on the lake when a dramatic storm begins (described in canto III of *CH*).

14–18 B and his friends try their hands at composing ghost stories. (Shelley and Claire soon abandon their attempts, as does B, though Polidori's *The Vampyre*, published in 1819 [see 24 Apr 1819], perhaps owes something to B's attempts on this occasion. The most important outcome of the plan is Mary's *Frankenstein*, published in 1818.)

23   B and Shelley set off on a boat tour of the Lake of Geneva. (There is a detailed account of the tour in a journal letter written by Shelley to Peacock, published in *The Letters of Percy Bysshe Shelley*, pp. 430–8, and all quotations relating to the tour are from this source.) Leaving Montalegre at 2.30 p.m., they arrive 'after three hours of rowing' at Hermance, then continue to Nernier, a 'remote and romantic village', where they walk by the lake and spend the night.

24   They continue to Evian via Yvoire.

25 To St Gingolph via Meillerie; the route affords views of 'mighty forests which overhung the lake, and lawns of exquisite verdure, and mountains with bare and icy points'.

26 They sail to Clarens, visiting the Castle of Chillon, 'its dungeons and towers', *en route*.

27 They visit the castle at Clarens, then sail to Ouchy, 'a village near Lausanne', via Vevey.

28 They are detained at Ouchy by the rain and spend the time visiting Lausanne, where they see Gibbon's house and 'the decayed summer-house where he finished his History'; B 'gathered some acacia leaves [from the terrace] to preserve in remembrance of him' (on the same day he sends some acacia leaves and rose leaves from Gibbon's garden to Murray). B writes to Murray, telling him that the third canto of *CH* is completed. At about this time he composes *The Prisoner of Chillon*.

29–30 They leave Ouchy on the 29th and 'after two days of pleasant sailing arrived on Sunday evening [30th] at Montalegre'.

July

7 (Sun) Death of Sheridan. At Kinnaird's request, B writes a 'Monody' to be read at Drury Lane Theatre and sends it to Kinnaird on the 20th (a revised version is sent on the 22nd).

17 In a letter to Peacock, Shelley describes B as 'an exceedingly interesting person', but adds, 'as such is it not to be regretted that he is a slave to the vilest and most vulgar prejudices, and as mad as the winds'.

22 B tells Murray that he has heard of Lady Caroline Lamb's novel *Glenarvon* (published 9 May), but has not yet seen it (the hero of the novel is closely based on B).

29 Tells Rogers that he has read Constant's *Adolphe* and found it 'leaves an unpleasant impression'. During this period B frequently visits Madame de Staël, who is depicted in the novel and who lives at Coppet.

August

14 (Wed) Matthew ('Monk') Lewis arrives at the Villa Diodati.

16 B and Lewis make an excursion to Voltaire's house at Ferney.

26 Hobhouse and Davies arrive.

28 B says goodbye to Shelley, Mary and Claire, who are leaving

for England. Shelley carries with him the manuscript of canto III of *CH* and that of *PC* for delivery to Murray (his appearance with these manuscripts in Murray's office on 11 Sep causes the publisher to be 'thrilled with delight': Murray to B, 12 Sep). Claire is pregnant with B's child; before she leaves, she writes to him asking him to write to her ('My dreadful fear is lest you quite forget me'). Later she recalls that, before they parted, B withdrew, at her urging, his earlier suggestion that the child should be placed 'under the protection of Mrs [Augusta] Leigh' and promised that it 'should never be away from one of its parents' (letter of 21 Mar 1821). (For the birth of the child, see 12 Jan 1817.)

29   B, Davies and Hobhouse set off on an excursion to Chamonix and Mont Blanc. In the guest-book of an inn at which Shelley has stayed, B finds, and erases, Shelley's inscription in Greek (translation: 'Democrat, great lover of mankind, and atheist').

September

1   (Sun) Back at the Villa Diodati. Hobhouse notes in his diary that 'B has given me another canto of *CH* to read'.

4   Hobhouse talks to B about the latter's affairs until midnight.

5   Davies and Rushton depart for England, Davies carrying with him gifts from B for Ada and for Augusta and her children.

7   B and Hobhouse go to Geneva; B visits Madame de Staël again at about this time.

8   Tells Augusta that he is in good health, but that the separation has 'broken my heart'.

16   B and Hobhouse visit Geneva again. Polidori is dismissed at about this time.

17–29   B and Hobhouse visit the Bernese Oberland. B keeps an 'Alpine Journal', intended for Augusta and recording the route and sights in detail (B describes it as a 'record of what I have seen and felt': it is printed in *L&J*, v, 96–105; another account is given in Hobhouse's *Recollections*, II, 17–24; quotations are from the former.)

17   They set off at 7 a.m., see 'Mont Blanc – and the Aiguille of Argentière both very distinct', reach Lausanne before sunset, and spend the night at Ouchy.

18   They travel to Clarens via Vevey, and visit the Castle of Chillon.

19 'Crossed the mountains to Montbovon on horseback – and on Mules . . . .'
20 '. . . the whole of this day's journey at an average of between from two thousand seven hundred to three thousand feet above the level of the Sea.'
21 They see the Lake of Thun and visits the Château de Schadau.
22 From Thoun by boat, a three-hour journey to Neuhause via Interlaken; they arrive 'at the foot of the [Jungfrau]', hear an avalanche, see a glacier, and are caught in a storm.
23 Their Alpine journey continues, 'Avalanches falling every five minutes nearly', and B throws a snowball at Hobhouse.
24 Among other sights, they see the Reichenbach waterfall and descend to the Lake of Brientz.
25 They leave Brientz and are rowed on the lake to Interlaken, where they dine; then on the Lake of Thun to Thun.
26 To Fribourg via Berne.
27 They visit the cathedral at Fribourg, then proceed to Yverdun.
28 To Aubonne, and enjoy a fine view of the Lake of Geneva.
29 Back at the Villa Diodati, where B finds a letter from Murray saying that Gifford has praised canto III of *CH* highly (on receiving the manuscript, Murray has taken it at once to Gifford, who, despite illness, has sat up reading it that night until he has finished it). On the 27th Claire has written to B that she loves him 'more and more every day'.
30 B suffers a minor injury while boating.
Begins *Manfred* during this month.

October

1 (Tues) Dines with Madame de Staël.
5 B and Hobhouse set off on a tour of Italy, travelling via the Simplon Pass and Lake Maggiore (again, Hobhouse's *Recollections* provide a detailed account).
6 Hobhouse notes in his diary that, after he has retired for the night, 'Byron called me out to look at the rocks and the church and the snow-tops of the Dent du Midi, sleeping in the moonlight . . . .' Claire writes to B that she recognises some of the speeches in Lady Caroline Lamb's *Glenarvon* (see 22 July) as his, or characteristic of him.
10 B and Hobhouse arrive in Ornavasso; before setting off the next morning, they make (according to Hobhouse) 'every arrangement for battle' in case of encountering robbers on the

road: they have 'four brace of pistols in our carriage, two swords, two sword-sticks, and Byron's dagger', and the guide and the postillion are both armed.

12   They arrive in Milan. B engages in extensive sightseeing and socialising, and meets Stendhal, Vincenzo Monti (Italian poet) and other literary figures.

15   They visit the Ambrosian Library in Milan and see autograph letters of Lucrezia Borgia and 'A long lock of her bright yellow hair' (Hobhouse); according to Hobhouse, B 'has taken the hair'.

17   They go to the theatre and see Monti there.

20   Stendhal tells a correspondent that he has dined with B at Monsieur de Brême's, having met him for the first time at La Scala theatre on the previous day; Monti is also present at the dinner. Stendhal sees B frequently thereafter, and later records B's expressions of his admiration for Napoleon.

28   Polidori, who is in Milan, is arrested for insulting an Austrian officer at La Scala; B's efforts to extricate him from his difficulties are in vain, and Polidori is expelled from the city the next day.

30   Shelley tells Murray that B has asked him to 'revise the proofs' of canto III of *CH* and *PC*.

November

1   (Fri) B writes to his wife, refers to his 'great capacity for suffering', and tells her that he would willingly be reunited with her if it were possible. He also says that he may 'perhaps' visit England the following spring.

3   B and Hobhouse leave Milan for Venice; they travel via Verona (where they visit the amphitheatre and Juliet's tomb), Vicenza and Padua, and reach Venice on the 10th.

11   Writes to Hanson complaining of reports that Lady Byron intends to take or send Ada to the Continent, and asking him to prevent this, if necessary by legal action. The letter also refers to an intended return to England the following spring.

17   Tells Moore that he is studying Armenian at a monastery. At this time B falls in love with Marianna Segati; he reports to Kinnaird on the progress of their affair on the 27th.

18   Canto III of *CH* is published in London.

22   Scott, who has been reading canto III of *CH*, comments (in a letter to J. B. S. Morritt) on 'the powerful and ruined mind' of

B, and predicts that he may end in 'suicide or utter insanity';
four days later he writes to Joanna Baillie in similar terms,
remarking that the poem 'intimates a terrible state of mind'.
(On his review of the poem, see 11 Feb 1817.)

December
4   (Wed) B tells Moore that Marianna and the Armenian alphabet
    will between them 'last [him] the winter' (for the allusions,
    see 17 Nov).
5   Publication of *The Prisoner of Chillon and Other Poems* in
    London. Hobhouse leaves Venice to tour Italy.
8   Shelley tells Hunt that B 'expressed . . . the high esteem
    which he felt for your character & worth'.
18 A letter to Augusta reveals B as in high spirits; he refers to his
    wife as a 'virtuous monster' and to the 'tortures' of the past
    two years, but states that he has been 'very tranquil' for the
    past month.
26 Dines with the Countess Albrizzi and afterwards goes to the
    opera. B's Armenian studies continue. The Carnival begins in
    Venice.

1817

January
10 (Fri) Sending his review of canto III of *CH* to Murray,
    Scott writes, 'You know how high I hold [B's] poetical
    reputation . . . .'
12 Birth of Allegra, illegitimate daughter of B and Claire
    Clairmont, in Bath (in a letter to Kinnaird on the 20th, B
    refers to Claire's pregnancy and states his belief that the child
    is his).
22 B's twenty-ninth birthday.
28 Advises Moore to diet, as he himself has done for some time.
    He is still thinking of visiting England in the spring.
During this month, B participates in the Venice Carnival, which
continues until 18 February.

February
11 (Tues) *Quarterly Review* (issue dated Oct 1816) appears,
    containing Scott's review of *CH* canto III.

15 B tells Murray that he has finished a blank-verse drama in three acts (i.e. *Manfred*, begun in Switzerland the previous Sep). He sends the first act to Murray on 28 February and the other two acts early in March with a request to seek the opinion of Gifford and others as to the quality of the work. (See also 14 Apr.)

25 Reports himself to Murray as slightly unwell as a result of late nights and dissipation. Tells Murray that he intends to write a tragedy on the subject of the Falieri.

28 Tells Moore that he is on an invalid diet following his dissipation during the Carnival.

March

10 (Mon) Tells Moore that he has been ill with a low fever. On the 25th he tells him that he has had a week of sleeplessness, 'half-delirium', and other symptoms, but has now recovered (without, as he boasts to many friends, the aid of a physician).

31 Tells Hobhouse that he has been reading Voltaire, and has bought a complete set of his works in 92 volumes.

April

14 (Mon) Having corrected the proofs of *Manfred*, B decides that Act III is 'd——d bad'; he rewrites it after he reaches Rome on the 29th and sends it to Murray on 5 May.

17 Sets off for Rome, travelling via Ferrara, Bologna and Florence.

22 In Florence, where he spends only one day, he visits art galleries and returns 'drunk with beauty' (to Murray, 26 Feb).

23 Shelley writes to Byron asking what his plans are for Allegra and telling him that he and Mary would be pleased to take care of the child during B's absence abroad.

29 B arrives in Rome, where he stays at 66 Piazza di Spagna.

May

5 (Mon) Tells Murray that he is 'riding all about the country'.

9 Tells Murray that he has read Scott's *Tales of my Landlord* 'with great pleasure', and that his health is very good. In Rome, accompanied by Hobhouse, he sees all the tourist sights and rides daily.

10 Dines with Lord Lansdowne.

19 Witnesses a public execution (three robbers are guillotined)

and finds the effect 'very striking and chilling' (the incident is vividly described in a letter to Murray on 30 May).

20 Leaves Rome. Hobhouse proceeds to Naples, but B decides not to accompany him in view of the large number of English tourists there. (Hobhouse returns to Venice at the end of July.)

27 In Florence on the way back to Venice.

28 Back in Venice.

While in Rome during this month, B sits for a bust by Bertel Thorvaldsen, Danish sculptor.

June

4 (Wed) Takes a six-month lease of the Villa Foscarini at La Mira, on the banks of the Brenta, near Venice.

14 Tells Hanson that he is anxious for Newstead to be sold. Tells Augusta that he will not return to England unless business demands it.

16 Publication of *Manfred*.

26 Begins the fourth canto of *CH*; by 1 July (letter to Murray), he has written more than thirty stanzas; by 15 July (to Murray) 98 stanzas have been drafted. See also 20 July below.

July

During this month John Wilson ('Christopher North') reviews *Manfred* in *Blackwood's Magazine*. Early in the month M. G. ('Monk') Lewis, who is in Venice, pays a visit to B.

20 (Sun) Tells Murray that he has completed canto IV of *CH* in 126 stanzas. On 17 September, however, telling Murray that Hobhouse will bring the manuscript when he travels to England, B gives its length as 150 stanzas.

31 Hobhouse rejoins B at La Mira; Lewis and Marianna Segati are also there at this time.

August

12 (Tues) Tells Murray that he has been very sorry to hear of the death of Madame de Staël (she died in Paris on 14 July).

During this month B meets Margarita Cogni (see 1 Aug 1819).

September

In the latter part of the month, Kinnaird and his brother (Lord Kinnaird) arrive in Venice and spend some time with B. During this month B meets R. B. Hoppner. In the issue of the *Edinburgh Review* that appears this month (dated Aug), Jeffrey reviews *Manfred* favourably.

14 (Sun) B talks to Hobhouse 'about family matters', and Hobhouse records in his diary that B 'does not care about his wife now – that is certain'.

October

12 (Sun) Thanks Murray for sending Jeffrey's review of *Manfred* (see Sep); the letter also refers to the 'very good' review of the same work by John Wilson (see July).

14 'Found Byron well, and merry and happy, more charming every day' (Hobhouse).

20 Sees Ticknor again, according to whom B tells him, as he is leaving, that 'he should see me in America in a couple of years'.

23 Tells Murray that he has completed *Beppo*, which is based on an anecdote heard on 29 August.

November

1 (Sat) Visits Este to see a country house he has leased for two years from Hoppner.

6 Death of Princess Charlotte, daughter of the Prince Regent and subject of B's poem 'To a Lady Weeping'.

13 Returns to Venice, the lease of the Villa Foscarini being nearly expired.

22 Goes to the Lido with Hobhouse, and they gallop along the beach.

23 B tells Hobhouse of the death of Princess Charlotte (see 6 Nov), news of which has just reached him, and both are 'really affected' (Hobhouse).

December

10 (Wed) Hears from Hanson that the Newstead estate has been sold for £94,500 to Thomas Wildman, whom B had known at Harrow.

13 B is unwell; Hobhouse sits at home with him.

14 B and Hobhouse discuss Hume, whom the latter has been reading. In the evening they go to the theatre.

1818

January

7   (Wed) Hobhouse rides with B, and spends the evening with him; they part at midnight.

8   Hobhouse sets off for England with the manuscript of canto IV of *CH* for delivery to Murray; B sends with it the verse epistle beginning 'My dear Mr Murray', which includes a promise to send *Beppo* when it has been copied.

19 Sends the manuscript of *Beppo* to Murray, telling him that it is 'full of political allusions' and must be published anonymously.

22 B's thirtieth birthday. He meets the Countess Guicciolo for the first time (see 6 Apr 1819).

27 Tells Murray that the Carnival is in full swing and that he has embarked on 'a new intrigue'.

February

2   (Mon) Commiserates with Moore on the death of his daughter, and declares his love for his own two daughters. B is throwing himself wholeheartedly into the dissipations of the Carnival, but is also riding several miles daily.

20 Tells Murray that he has been unwell for the past eight days.

21 Sees Rossini's opera *Othello*.

28 *Beppo* is published anonymously.

March

3   (Tues) Tells Hobhouse that he is suffering from gonorrhea, caught from Elena da Mosta.

5   Sends Murray corrections for *Beppo* and (on the 9th) three additional stanzas, with a further stanza on the 11th (B evidently does not know that the poem has already appeared).

25 Is negotiating with Count Gritti to rent the Palazzo Gritti on the Grand Canal for two years (the agreement does not materialise); see also 19 May below.

April

6   (Mon) Death of Lady Melbourne. B tells Murray on the 23rd that he feels only 'numbness' at the news, though she was 'the best & kindest & ablest female I ever knew'.

24 Tells Hobhouse that Shelley has gone to Milan with Claire and Allegra.

28   Publication of canto IV of *CH*.

May
 2   (Sat) Allegra and her nurse arrive in Venice and stay with the
     Hoppners.
19   B tells Hobhouse that his affair with Marianna Segati came to
     an end three months ago, but that there has been 'a world of
     other harlotry'. He has rented the Palazzo Mocenigo on the
     Grand Canal for three years at £200 per annum.

June
Early in the month B moves into the Palazzo Mocenigo and is
joined there by Allegra and her nurse. He retains his villa in the
Euganean hills for summer use. At about this time Giovanni
Falcieri (nicknamed Tita) becomes B's gondolier.
25   (Mon) Tells Hobhouse that he has recently been involved in a
     swimming-contest with two friends, Angelo Mengaldo and
     Alexander Scott: they have raced from the Lido to the end of
     the Grand Canal, and B has won by three-quarters of a mile
     after being in the water continuously for $3\frac{3}{4}$ hours.

July
 3   (Fri) Begins *Don Juan*.
10   Tells Murray that he is still waiting for Hanson's cheque to
     arrive together with the papers for signature in order to
     complete the sale of Newstead (the business has been
     dragging on for months: see also 30 Sep); also that he is
     thinking of writing his memoirs, and that he has two tales,
     'one serious & one ludicrous' (possibly *Mazeppa* and *DJ*), in
     progress.

August
 3   (Mon) Tells Augusta that Allegra has been with him for three
     months and is a very attractive child.
22   Shelley and Claire arrive in Venice at midnight (one of several
     brief visits by one or other of them during this period).
23   Shelley calls on B at 3 p.m. and they discuss Allegra's future,
     then proceed in B's gondola to the Lido: 'Our conversation
     consisted in histories of his wounded feelings, & questions as
     to my affairs, & great professions of friendship & regard for
     me' (Shelley to Mary Shelley, 23 Aug); they also talk of

'literary matters' and B repeats stanzas from canto IV of *CH*. Shelley and B ride on the Lido – a ride commemorated in Shelley's *Julian and Maddalo, A Conversation* (written 1818, published 1824). Later Shelley tells Peacock that on this visit he 'hardly knew' B – 'he is changed into the liveliest, & happiest looking man I ever met' (letter of 8 Oct).

24 Shelley tells his wife that he is concealing from B the news of Claire's presence in Venice, as Hoppner has told him that B 'often expresses his extreme horror of her arrival, and the necessity which it would impose on him of instantly quitting Venice'.

26 B tells Murray that the memoirs (see 10 July) are 'nearly finished': they have turned out longer than he anticipated and he will not publish them for the time being, but will keep them among his papers.

September

8 (Tues) Writes to Webster about his love of Venice – 'all its disadvantages are more than compensated by the sight of a single Gondola' – and his living-costs there (about £5000 in two years, more than half of which has been spent on women).

19 Tells Moore that he has finished the first canto of *DJ* ('about 180' stanzas are written, but the canto eventually contains 222): he has been encouraged to do so by the success of *Beppo*. (Murray has told him in a letter of 16 June that he has already sold 3000 copies of the latter, even though its authorship is not yet public knowledge, and Jeffrey has praised it in the *Edinburgh Review* as 'extremely clever and amusing').

21 Tells Augusta that Claire has recently arrived and caused an uproar among his 'venetian loves'; he has therefore packed her and Allegra off to his country villa for a month.

24–9 Shelley and his wife visit B, who reads to Shelley canto I of *DJ*.

30 Writes to Hanson, who is in Geneva but refuses to come to Venice; the sale of Newstead is still uncompleted (see also 11 November below).

In the issue of the *Quarterly Review* that appears during this month, but is dated April, Scott reviews canto IV of *CH*.

October

9 (Fri) Moore notes in his journal that he has received a long letter from B containing 'two stanzas of the Beppo-ish poem he is about, called "Don Juan"'.

12 B sends to Augusta miniatures of himself and Allegra.

November

11 (Wed) Hanson at last arrives in Venice with the papers for the sale of Newstead. B tells Hobhouse that the satirical dedication of *DJ* to Southey was prompted by the latter's calumny in referring to the 'League of Incest' formed by B and Shelley (B points out that Mary Godwin and Claire Clairmont were not sisters but step-sisters, and that moreover he had no sexual relations with the former).

17 B signs a codicil to his will providing a legacy of £5000 for his daughter Allegra; afterwards he plays billiards and exchanges reminiscences of Harrow with a visitor named Townsend; Newton Hanson (son of B's lawyer) notes that he is 'in the highest spirits' but 'persistently biting his nails'.

18 Hanson has submitted his bill for legal services, without details; it amounts to over £9000. B has agreed to pay him £5000. Hanson leaves Venice on the 19th.

24 B tells Murray that he is willing for his attack on Southey, whom he describes as a 'burning liar', to be made public.

28 Moore notes in his journal that, in a conversation with Davies, Moore's intended challenge to B early in 1810 has been discussed; Moore has told Davies 'that Lord B. had said since he never meant to fire at me' [i.e. would not have used a loaded pistol if it had come to a duel], and notes that 'Lord B.'s conduct on this occasion was full of manliness and candour'. (Moore's complaint had followed a slighting reference in *EBSR* to his duel with Jeffrey in 1806 [see 1 Jan 1810]; since B had already left England, however, the quarrel was confined to an acrimonious exchange of letters, the challenge seems never to have been issued, and on B's return the idea of a duel was not revived.)

December

13 (Sun) Begins canto II of *DJ*.

22 Shelley writes to Peacock concerning B's moral degeneration: 'He allows fathers and mothers to bargain with him for their

daughters. He associates with wretches who seem almost to have lost the gait and physiognomy of man, and who do not scruple to avow practices which are not only not named, but I believe seldom even conceived in England. He says he disapproves, but he endures.' He also writes to Hunt in a similar vein: 'Our poor friend Lord Byron is quite corrupted by living among these people . . .'; and he tells Hunt that B is eager for him to come to Italy and will lend him four or five hundred pounds for travelling-expenses if necessary.

27 Hobhouse notes in his diary that he and Davies breakfasted together and read the first canto of *DJ* and other poems by B in manuscript: Hobhouse has 'doubts' about *DJ*. Two days later he calls on Hookham Frere, who is 'decisively against publication'. On 9 January 1819 Hobhouse writes to B advising him not to publish; Murray and others see the letter and agree with it, the reasons being 'the attacks on the wife' and 'the bawdry and the blasphemy'. Moore agrees with their views, but later insists on publication.

1819

January
19 (Tues) Tells Hobhouse and Kinnaird that he will not allow *DJ* to be cut on moral grounds; he has finished the second canto but it awaits copying.
22 B's thirty-first birthday.
25 Instructs Murray to print fifty copies of canto ɪ of *DJ* for private circulation. Tells Hobhouse that he is willing not to have the poem published (Hobhouse, Kinnaird, Davies and other friends in England have advised him that it would give offence).
27 Tells Kinnaird that the decision not to publish *DJ* will cost him 'thousands of pounds'.
28 Rogers tells Moore that *DJ* 'is pronounced by Hobhouse and others as unfit for publication'; Moore comments in his journal that this judgement is 'too true'.
During this month B is ill with stomach trouble.

February
1 (Mon) Sends Murray an additional stanza for *DJ* (and other additions at other times during this period).

16 The money from the sale of Newstead is paid.

22 Tells Murray that he has been involved in the Carnival, which finishes the next day, and has not been to bed until 7 or 8 a.m. for the past ten days. Tells Kinnaird that he will publish *DJ*, as he needs the money; and reaffirms this intention on 6 March, declaring then that he will not 'flatter' public opinion.

April

3 (Sat) Sends Murray the second canto of *DJ* and instructs him to publish the first two cantos without omissions.

6 Mary Shelley writes to Hunt from Rome, 'all goes on as badly [in Venice] with the noble poet as ever I fear – he is a lost man if he does not escape soon'. B tells Hobhouse that he has fallen in love with a nineteen-year-old countess from Ravenna (Teresa Guiccioli) who is married to a man in his fifties. (B had met her for the first time at the Albrizzi's in Jan 1818, and they met again at the Countess Benzoni's on 2 or 3 Apr 1818. His references to the ages of Teresa and her husband vary: to Kinnaird on 24 Apr she is 'twenty' and he 'sixty'.) Their affair develops rapidly.

12 or 13 Teresa leaves for Ravenna with her husband (see also 17 May); B receives three letters from her and writes to her (in Italian) on the 22nd and 23rd.

24 Tells Kinnaird that he is 'damnably in love', and describes Teresa as 'the queerest woman I ever met with'. The same letter contains B's impatient reaction to rumours that he is the author of Polidori's *The Vampyre*, recently published anonymously and widely ascribed to B. On the 27th he writes to the editor of *Galignani's Messenger* contradicting the report.

27 Mary Shelley writes to Maria Gisborne, 'What a miserable thing it is that [B] should be lost as he is among the worst inhabitants of Venise [*sic*]'.

May

15 (Sat) Returns a proof of the first two cantos of *DJ* to Murray, and instructs him to publish it anonymously and without the dedication. He also tells Murray that he will probably leave Venice shortly.

17 Tells Augusta that he has never ceased to love her and is 'utterly incapable of *real* love for any other human being'.

(Augusta subsequently forwards the letter to B's wife with the comment that 'He is surely to be considered a *Maniac*.') Tells Hobhouse that Teresa was pregnant when their affair began and has miscarried during the journey to Ravenna. Early in the morning of the 18th, B slips while getting into his gondola and falls into the Grand Canal on his way to an assignation with a nobleman's daughter named Angelina.

June

1   (Tues) Leaves Venice in order to visit Teresa in Ravenna; he plans to be away for about a month.
2   In Padua.
3   In Ferrara: sight-seeing and social engagements.
6   In Bologna: more sight-seeing.
10 In Ravenna, where he finds that Teresa has been very ill following her miscarriage (see 17 May).
20 Tells Hoppner that he is not likely to return to Venice for some time. His affair with Teresa continues; Count Guiccioli is a frequent visitor and takes B out in his carriage.
21 Writes the dedicatory sonnet to *The Prophecy of Dante*.
26 Tells Hobhouse that Teresa is still very weak.
28 Publication of *Mazeppa* and the 'Ode on Venice'.
29 Tells Alexander Scott that Teresa is 'seriously ill' and consumption is feared.

July

15 (Thurs) Publication of cantos I and II of *DJ*; the title-page bears no indication of author or publisher.
20 Tells Lady Byron that he has had no news of his daughter Ada for a long time.
24 Tells Scott that he has decided not to return to Venice, and that the Guicciolis have played no part in this decision.
26 Tells Augusta that to him she will always be 'the first consideration in the World': since she is ill, he is prepared to visit England to be with her or to pay her and her family's expenses to enable them to come to Venice. He also tells her, at length, about his affair with Teresa, and mentions his flirtation with Teresa's friend, Geltruda Vicari.

August

During this month *Blackwood's Magazine* reviews *DJ* (cantos I and II).

1   (Sun) Gives Murray, evidently at his request, a long account
    of his affair, which lasted for two years (i.e. since Aug 1819),
    with Margarita Cogni, the illiterate wife of a Venetian baker
    (and hence nicknamed 'La Fornarina').

9   Tells Murray that his affiar with Teresa has involved 'perils'
    and 'escapes' in comparison with which those of his hero
    Don Juan are 'child's play'.

10 Leaves for Bologna, where the Guicciolis have gone the
    previous day.

11 Attends a performance of Alfieri's tragedy *Mirra* and is greatly
    moved by it. Two weeks later he tells Murray that he has not
    been well since the performance.

16 Peterloo massacre takes place in Manchester.

20 Tells Hobhouse that he is passing the time in Bologna
    'viciously and agreeably', and that he is thinking of going to
    settle in South America.

22 Receives from Murray a review of *DJ* that has appeared in the
    British Review.

At the end of this month Allegra arrives to stay with her father;
soon afterwards he tells Augusta that she can speak only Italian,
in the Venetian dialect.

September

12 (Sun) With Teresa, whose husband has returned to Ravenna
    on business, B sets off for Venice. When they reach Padua,
    they consider eloping to France or America; but at B's urging
    the idea is abandoned. On arrival in Venice, they stay at his
    country house, La Mira.

October

3   (Sun) B mentions the South American project (see 20 Aug)
    again to Hobhouse; this time Venezuela is referred to, and B
    evidently has permanent settlement in mind. In a letter to
    Webster two days later, his intention of taking Allegra with
    him is stated.

7   Moore arrives at La Mira at 2 p.m. on a visit to Byron and
    finds B 'but just up and in his bath' (Moore's accounts of his
    reception are excerpted in *I&R*, pp. 58–62). During dinner,
    according to Moore's journal, they have 'much curious
    conversation' about B's wife, and also discuss *DJ*.

8   Moore and 'Mr [Alexander] Scott' dine with B.

9   The three dine together again; after dinner, B reads to Moore 'what he has done of the third canto of "Don Juan"' (Moore's journal); then they all go to the opera and afterwards to 'a sort of public-house, to drink hot punch'. B takes Moore home in his gondola at 2 a.m.

11 Moore visits B again and has 'a handsome dinner': 'He has given me his Memoirs to make what use I please of them' (Moore's journal). (See also 29th.) He says goodbye to B (they never meet again).

22 B tells Hoppner that he is thinking of going to England in the spring.

26 Tells Kinnaird that he has 'not had a whore this half-year' but has confined himself to 'the strictest adultery'; that he is still interested in the idea of emigrating to South America; and that he has written 'about a hundred' stanzas of canto III of *DJ*.

28 Tells Hoppner that he has heard from Murray that the first two cantos of *DJ* have not sold well (in another letter to Hoppner the next day he states that 1200 out of 1500 have been sold). B hears from Murray that a spurious *Don Juan, Canto the Third* by William Hone has appeared in London.

29 Tells Murray that after B's death he may 'do what you please' with the memoirs and other autobiographical material that he has given to Moore, and in the meantime may read them and circulate them in manuscript if he wishes; their publication is, however, expressly forbidden until after B's death. (At this stage, the memoirs recount B's life only as far as 1816; subsequently B continues the memoirs and sends the additional material to Moore. For the later fate of the work, see 2 and 7 Jan 1820; Nov 1820; 14 and 17 May 1824.)

31 Leigh Hunt reviews cantos I and II of *DJ* in *The Examiner*.

November

1   (Mon) Count Guiccioli arrives at the Palazzo Mocenigo with the intention of taking Teresa back to Ravenna. They leave about ten days later.

8   B tells Murray that he has been ill for a week or more with fever after being drenched in a thunderstorm while out riding on 28 October; and that about 110 stanzas of *DJ* (canto III) and about 500 lines of *The Prophecy of Dante* have been written.

16 Tells Kinnaird that he and Allegra will go to England in a few

weeks. He intends to leave Italy on account of Teresa, whose husband has quarrelled with her and delivered an ultimatum, and he is still hoping to go eventually to America or South America. He has not yet fully recovered from the fever noted under 8 November; in a postscript written on the 17th he mentions that he has had another attack, and that Allegra is also ill – a development that causes the planned return to England to be postponed.

28 B is now well, but Allegra is still ill with fever.
30 Finishes canto III of *DJ*.

December
 2 (Thurs) Tells Teresa that he is leaving Italy for her sake and will go to England.
 4 Tells Augusta that he will be setting out in a few days and expects to be 'in or near England by the new year'. Tells Murray that canto III of *DJ* is finished and consists of about 200 stanzas.
10 Tells Kinnaird that in view of the season and Allegra's still imperfect health, he has postponed his journey to England and intends instead to go to Ravenna.
21 Leaves Venice.
23 In Bologna.
24 Arrives in Ravenna, where he finds Teresa again ill.
31 Writes to Lady Byron referring to recent events and to his memoirs.

1820

January
 2 (Sun) Tells Moore that Lady Byron may, if she wishes, see the memoirs. The Carnival is about to begin.
 7 Moore tells Murray that B has made him 'the very precious gift of his memoirs': Murray may read them, but they must not be published until 'the end of the nineteenth century'.
22 B's thirty-second birthday.
29 Death of George III; he is succeeded by the Prince Regent as George IV.

February
1 (Mon) Tells Murray that he has divided canto III of *DJ* into two cantos on account of its length; he is doubtful about the wisdom of publishing them because they lack the 'Spirit' of the earlier cantos. It has been very cold in Ravenna, with frost and snow, but is now mild again.
19 Sends cantos III and IV of *DJ* to Murray and tells him that, as far as payment is concerned, they are to count as a single canto. He declines Murray's invitation to write 'a volume of manners &c. – on Italy'.
20 Tells Lady Byron that he will not attend the Coronation, and asks for a picture of Ada to be sent to him.
21 Finishes his translation of the first canto of Luigi Pulci's *Morgante Maggiore*, and sends it to Murray at the end of the month.
26 Tells Bankes that he has enjoyed reading more of Scott's novels (he has correctly guessed the authorship of these anonymous works).

March
1 (Wed) Asks Murray to send him Scott's latest novels and says that they are his favourite reading.
Early in the month Teresa quarrels with B.
10 B is involved in a carriage accident but escapes with bruises.
14 Sends his *Prophecy of Dante*, recently completed, to Murray.
In the second half of the month, B writes his prose 'Observations upon an Article in *Blackwood's Magazine*' in response to the 'Remarks on *Don Juan*' published in that magazine in August 1819, which describe it as a 'filthy and impious poem'. The 'Observations' are sent to Murray on 28 March and circulated by him in manuscript, but not published during B's lifetime.
28 Tells Murray that he is thinking of publishing his *Hints from Horace*, written in 1811 (in the event the work is not published until after B's death).

April
9 (Sun) Tells Murray that he has begun 'a tragedy on the subject of Marino Faliero'.
22 Tells Hoppner that he intends to retain custody of Allegra, since he disapproves of the upbringing she would receive at

the hands of her mother. Congratulates Hobhouse on his election to Parliament.

During this month B's interest in the political situation in Italy increases as a crisis seems to approach: on the 30th he tells Kinnaird, 'we expect a rising'.

May

8   (Mon) Tells Murray that he is working on the second act of *MF*.

15   Tells Harriette Wilson that he is in a 'scrape' – a reference to the situation that has arisen after Count Guiccioli has caught B and Teresa 'quasi in the fact' (to Murray, 20 May). B is warned to be on his guard against hired ruffians, and Teresa's father, Count Gamba, seeks the Pope's permission for a separation between his daughter and her husband.

19   Claire notes in her journal that she receives 'A Brutal Letter' from B.

June

1   (Thurs) Tells Moore that 'The separation business [see 15 May above] still continues', and that public opinion is against Count Guiccioli for raising objections to the affair after countenancing it for a year.

7   Thanks Murray for sending Scott's *Ivanhoe*.

9   Tells Moore that he is working on the third act of *MF*.

22   Tells Hobhouse that cantos III and IV of *DJ* must be published anonymously, since if his authorship were known 'in the present state of Cant and hypocrisy in England' he might be deprived, as Shelley was, of the guardianship of his own children.

July

2   (Sun) Revolt breaks out in Naples involving the Carbonari and other secret revolutionary societies; B follows the events with interest and in August is initiated into the Carbonari.

6   Tells Hobhouse that Teresa's separation is under consideration by the Pope; when the matter is settled, he will be able to decide whether to come to England.

13   Tells Moore that the Pope has granted the separation between Teresa and Count Guiccioli (B has received the news the previous day). The Count is to pay alimony of 1200 crowns

per annum – 'a handsome allowance', according to B (letter to Kinnaird, 20 July).

17 Tells Teresa that he has finished *MF* but now has to revise and copy it.
20 Tells Hoppner that he has been suffering from fever and is unwell.
25 Sends Act I of *MF* to Murray.
29 Tells Teresa that he likes her brother Pietro, whom he has recently met, very much.

August
 7 (Mon) Tells Murray that he has now sent three acts of *MF* and is copying the rest (he sends Act IV on the 12th and the last act on the 17th).
18 The *Morning Chronicle* announces, erroneously, B's arrival in London.
24 Sends Teresa a copy of Constant's *Adolphe* and praises its truth; she obviously reads it at once and takes exception to what she supposes to be B's motives in sending it to her, for on the 26th he reassures her that their own situation is quite different from that depicted in the novel, which deals with the tormented love affair of a young man for an older married woman.
28 Sends Murray revisions to *MF*; further revisions follow on 31 August and 16 October.
?30 Praises Richard Westall's illustrations to *DJ* as 'quite beautiful' (to Murray).
31 Tells Hoppner that Allegra has been ill but is recovering. Tells Kinnaird that *MF* is 'at least as good' as 'Mr Turdsworth's' [i.e. Wordsworth's] *Peter Bell* (published in 1819 and satirised by Shelley in his *Peter Bell the Third*, written in 1819 but not published until 1839; also parodied by J. H. Reynolds in *Peter Bell: A Lyrical Ballad* [1819], which B has read by this date and believes may be by Moore).

September
15 (Fri) Death of Ferdinando Guiccioli, stepson of Teresa.
21 B writes to Hobhouse concerning the Queen Caroline affair (a bill to dissolve her marriage to George IV has been introduced on 5 July but is dropped in November); he tells Hobhouse that in Ravenna 'nobody believes the evidence against the Queen'.

October

12   (Thurs) Thanks Murray for sending various books, including
      'Johnny Keats's *p–ss a bed* poetry' (i.e. his 1820 volume, which
      includes *The Eve of St Agnes*, *Lamia* and other poems) and
      fiction by Hogg and others.

16   Begins canto v of *DJ* (see also 27 Nov, 14 and 28 Dec).

17   Sends Murray the dedication of *MF* (to Goethe), written on
      the 14th.

?18   Tells Augusta that Italy is 'a very distracted State'.

25   Writes to Lady Byron on business matters and also concerning
      his daughter Ada, a picture of whom he has received. He
      asks his wife to 'be kind' to Augusta and her children if
      anything should happen to him. Asks Murray to send him a
      copy of Scott's novel *The Monastery* (a letter to Hoppner on
      the 28th shows that he has already read Scott's *The Abbot*, the
      sequel to *The Monastery*).

November

During this month B composes additional material for his memoirs.

 4   (Sat) In a letter to Murray, B praises Pope as 'the most *faultless*
      of Poets, and almost of men', and attacks Keats ('his is the
      Onanism of Poetry'). (The occasion for his remarks is provided
      by articles in the *Quarterly Review* and the *Edinburgh Review*.)

18   In a letter to Murray, B again refers to Keats in opprobrious
      terms.

27   Finishes canto v of *DJ*.

December

 9   (Sat) In the evening, the 'commandant of the troops' in
      Ravenna is shot dead near B's house: B takes charge of the
      situation and has the body carried into the house, then
      recounts the incident in letters to Moore and Murray (and,
      the next day, to Lady Byron).

14   Tells Murray that canto v of *DJ* is being copied; the copy is
      finished by the 26th.

28   Sends canto v of *DJ* to Kinnaird.

1821

January

2   (Tues) Tells Moore that he intends to remain in Ravenna until May or June, and refers to 'the Journal scheme' – i.e. the proposal to establish a newspaper, for which B suggests the title *The Harp*, in conjunction with Moore.

4   Begins his 'Ravenna Journal' (continued to 27 Feb), later abridged and published by Moore, who destroys the original. The diary for this day shows that B rose late 'as usual', ate a heavy dinner, read the newspapers, wrote five letters, visited Teresa in the evening, returned home before eleven o'clock, and read a biography of Leonardo da Vinci before writing his journal and going to bed.

13 Drafts an outline of his tragedy *Sardanapalus*, and writes the opening lines the next day.

20 Writes to the Lord Chamberlain to request his intervention to prevent unauthorised performances of *MF* (see also 25 Apr).

22 B's thirty-third birthday. At midnight on the 21st he goes to bed 'with a heaviness of heart at having lived so long, and to so little purpose' (*Journal*).

26 When returning home from riding, B meets an old woman; on asking her age, he learns that she is in her nineties. (He gives her a pension for life.)

February

10 (Sat) Completes the first of his letters on the Bowles–Pope controversy; it is sent to Murray and published by him later in the year. Tells Hoppner that he is going to send Allegra, whose disposition is 'perverse to a degree', to be educated in a convent.

14 Finishes Act I of *Sard.*

16 B's diary notes that he has recently purchased arms and ammunition for the Carbonari, a revolutionary group.

21 Writes a long letter to Murray concerning his swimming-feats in the Tagus, the Grand Canal and the Hellespont; the occasion of the letter, which is published in the *Monthly Magazine* and the *Traveller* in April, is some disparaging remarks on his swimming of the Hellespont which have appeared in William Turner's *Journal of a Tour in the Levant* (1820), published by Murray.

March

1 (Thurs) Allegra is sent to be educated at a convent in Bagnacavallo. Later in the month, Claire Clairmont writes a letter of protest to B, who defends his action in a letter to Hoppner on 3 April, in which he declares that he has spared neither 'trouble nor expense' in rearing the child and that he plans to have her brought up as a Roman Catholic ('which I look upon as the best religion as it is assuredly the oldest of the various branches of Christianity') and to provide her with a dowry. He again defends his action in a letter to Hoppner on 11 May, where he states that Allegra seems 'healthy & happy' in the convent.

April

21 (Sat) *MF* is published by Murray. B sends Murray a contribution for a fund in aid of the widow of John Scott, who had been one of B's schoolfellows at Aberdeen.

25 *MF* is produced at Drury Lane Theatre, in spite of B's wishes and without the permission of Murray, who has tried in vain to obtain an injunction from the Lord Chamberlain to prevent its staging. Six other performances follow, but it is not a marked success (see also 14 May).

26 Writes to Shelley expressing his regret at the death of Keats, who died in Rome on 23 February.

Southey's *The Vision of Judgement*, with a preface attacking the 'Satanic school' of poetry, appears during this month.

May

3 (Thurs) Tells Moore that he has always regarded Pope as 'the greatest name in our poetry'.

12 Tells Hodgson that he has recently spent more time on politics than on anything else.

14 Tells Murray that he has read in a Milan newspaper that *MF*, the production of which he has opposed in vain, has been performed and 'universally condemned' (an exaggerated report: see 25 Apr). The affair evidently irks B considerably, for he refers to it in several other letters at this time.

25 Tells Murray that he has finished four of the five acts of his tragedy *Sard*; the fifth act is written in the next two days. On the 28th he tells Kinnaird that it is *'not for the stage recollect always'*. He complains of the task of copying it, then evidently

decides against doing so, for the manuscript is sent to Murray on the 31st with the comment that he has 'retained no copy'.

June

12   (Tues) Begins *The Two Foscari*. As he tells Moore on 5 July, it is his 'third tragedy in twelve months'.

29   Tells Kinnaird that he has had stomach trouble for several days.

July

5   (Thurs) Is working on the fifth act of *TF*.

6   Tells Murray that, at Teresa's request, he has decided not to continue *DJ*.

10   Pietro Gamba, brother of Teresa, is arrested and sent into exile in Florence; within a day or two his father is also banished.

14   B returns the corrected proofs of *Sard* to Murray, and also sends him the manuscript of *TF*.

16   Begins *Cain*.

19   Coronation of George IV.

23   Tells Hoppner that, as a result of the political unrest and sending into exile of his friends, he has decided to move to Switzerland and is enquiring about a home on the Lake of Geneva (the idea is soon abandoned). Tells Kinnaird that Gifford has approved of *Sard*, but that Murray wishes to delay publication until the winter: B is pressing for immediate publication, before the theatres reopen for the winter season.

25   Teresa leaves Ravenna to join her father and brother in Florence.

30   Tells Murray that Keats's *Hyperion* is 'a fine monument & will keep his name'.

August

1   (Wed) In rescuing B's dog from under a mill-wheel, one Balani suffers a broken back; he dies on 12 August, and B bestows a pension on his widow.

2   Shelley, who is in Pisa, receives a letter from B inviting him to visit him in Ravenna; Shelley sets off the next day.

6   Shelley arrives in Ravenna and he and B sit up talking until five the next morning 'of poetry and such matters' (Shelley to his wife, 7 Aug). Shelley notes that B has 'completely

recovered his health, and lives a life totally the reverse of that which he led at Venice'. Shelley remains in Ravenna for about two weeks.

8   Murray publishes cantos III–V of *DJ*, with outstanding success.

10 Shelley tells his wife that B has read to him canto v of *DJ*: he judges it 'astonishingly fine'. He tells Peacock that B is 'in excellent cue both of health and spirits', and 'has got rid of all those melancholy and degrading habits which he indulged at Venice'. His account of B's day is that 'Lord Byron gets up at *two*. After breakfast we sit talking till six. From six till eight we gallop through the pine forests which divide Ravenna from the sea; we then come home and dine and sit up gossiping till six in the morning.'

11 Shelley tells his wife that B has 'decided upon coming to *Pisa*' and requires 'a large and magnificent house'.

16 B tells Teresa that he plans to take a house in Pisa with sufficient accommodation for her and her family as well as himself.

21 Shelley leaves Ravenna.

26 B tells Shelley that he is in 'all the agonies of packing' for the move to Pisa. Shelley tells Hunt that B has praised *Prometheus Unbound* and censured *The Cenci*; also that B 'is reformed, as far as gallantry goes, and lives with a beautiful and sentimental Italian lady, who is as much attached to him as may be. . . . He has many generous and exalted qualities, but the canker of aristocracy wants to be cut out . . . .' Shelley adds that B 'proposes that you should come out and go shares with him and me in a periodical work to be conducted here [i.e. *The Liberal*]'.

31 B tells Kinnaird that the new volume of *DJ* (see 8 Aug) is 'full of gross *misprints*', especially in the fifth canto. He has written to Murray 'very freely' on the subject, and asks Kinnaird and Hobhouse to compare the printed text with the manuscript, and to correct errors.

September

During this month B writes *A Vision of Judgement*.

9   (Sun) B is still involved in preparations for the move from Ravenna to Pisa.

10 Sends the manuscript of *Cain* to Murray.

13 Sends some of his hair to Augusta, to be placed in a locket for his daughter Ada.

14 Asks his wife to send him, via Augusta, some of Ada's hair (see 17 Nov); he also tells her that his experiments in writing tragedy are intended for 'the *mental* theatre of the reader', not for the stage. Shelley tells B that *The Prophecy of Dante* is 'indeed sublime', but that *DJ* is 'your greatest victory over the alleged inflexibility of your powers'. Shelley tells Horace Smith that B is expected in Pisa in 'about a fortnight' (but see 1 Nov); that he has 'just taken the finest palace in Pisa for [B]'; and that B is 'occupied in forming a new drama, and . . . is determined to write a series of plays, which will follow the French tragedians and Alfieri, rather than those of England and Spain, and produce something new, at least to England'.

19 B tells Moore that he has abandoned the idea of going to Greece with Pietro Gamba on account of Teresa's objections.

October

4 (Thurs) Sends the manuscript of *VJ* to Murray, to be published anonymously.

9 In a list of books which he requires Murray to send from England, B includes a Bible and remarks that as a young child he read the Old Testament 'through & through'. He also asks, among other items, for novels and poems by Scott, poems by Crabbe and Moore, and Burton's *Anatomy of Melancholy*.

15 Begins the journal *Detached Thoughts*.

22 Shelley tells John Gisborne that B is 'quite cured of his gross habits – as far as habits – the perverse ideas on which they were formed are not yet eradicated'.

28 B tells Murray that he is 'just setting off for Pisa'; in fact he leaves Ravenna the next day, and on the road to Bologna by chance meets Lord Clare, a Harrow schoolfriend. The night of the 29th is spent at Bologna; B meets Rogers there by arrangement, and they travel together as far as Florence.

During this month B writes *Heaven and Earth: A Mystery* (see 14 Dec).

November

1 (Thurs) B arrives in Pisa and settles in the Casa Lanfranchi, which he describes in a letter to Kinnaird on 20 November as

'a very good spacious house upon the Arno', and to Murray on 4 December as 'a famous old feudal palazzo'.

2   Shelley calls on B.

5   Shelley introduces Edward Williams to B; Williams notes in his journal B's 'unaffected and gentlemanly ease' and 'good humour', 'the elegance of his language and the brilliancy of his wit'. (For the next two months Williams' journal contains numerous references to B.)

6   B visits the Shelleys.

8   Mary Shelley rides with Teresa (one of numerous such outings during this period) and they meet B.

14   Shelley introduces Prince Argiropolo, a Greek exile related to Prince Mavrocordatos, to B. At about this time B also meets John Taaffe.

17   Thanks Lady Byron for sending him some of Ada's hair (see 13 Sep).

19   Williams calls on B and they have 'a long argument . . . on Women' (Williams' journal).

20   Shelley introduces Medwin to B, Medwin having arrived in Pisa on the 14th; he becomes a frequent companion of B's. (For Medwin's first impressions of B, see *I&R*, pp. 23–4.)

21   Medwin calls on B at 2 p.m. and finds him 'at breakfast, if it could be called one. It consisted of a cup of strong green tea, without milk or sugar, and an egg, of which he ate the yolk raw' (Medwin's *Conversations*).

30   Mary Shelley writes to Maria Gisborne: 'So here we live, Lord Byron just opposite to us in Casa Lanfranchi. . . . Shelley rides with him; I, of course, see little of him.'

December

2   (Sun) B and his companions shoot at a target (a favourite and frequent sport of B's): B hits the bull's-eye four times, 'and a half-crown piece three [times]', at a distance of fourteen yards (Williams' journal).

10   B notes in a letter to Murray that it is Ada's sixth birthday.

12   'S[helley] calls and tells us of having heard that a man was to be burnt alive at Lucca for sacrilege. He proposes that Lord B. and a party of English shall enter the town and rescue the man by force. Lord B. objects, but wishes to draw out a memorial to the Grand Duke of Tuscany to interfere' (Williams' journal). Taaffe goes to Lucca to make enquiries;

Mary Shelley notes in her journal on the 13th, 'Mr Taaffe calls. We find the burning story to be all false.'

14   B sends *H&E* to Murray, describing it (in a letter to Kinnaird) as 'a sort of Oratorio on a sacred subject'. In the evening, Shelley reads the poem aloud; recording the reading in his journal, Williams states that it was 'only finished the day before'.

17   Medwin, Shelley, Taaffe and Williams dine with B.

21   Begins *Werner*.

25   The same party as on the 17th dine with B. 'Before dinner, as we were sitting in [B's] studio, the conversation happening to turn on longevity, Byron offered Shelley a bet of £1000 on that of Lady Noel against Sir Timothy Shelley's, and which wager Shelley at once accepted' (Medwin, *Conversations*). Williams also records the wager in his journal.

28   Williams calls on B. Two days earlier, he has written to Trelawny that B is 'the very spirit of this place'.

1822

January

2   (Wed) Williams calls on B and they play at billiards with Shelley. Williams stays to dinner, at which Count Gamba and his son Pietro are also present, and hears of Polidori's suicide (he had taken poison at his London lodgings in August 1821).

3   Williams calls on B and finds him 'sitting for his bust to Bartolini' (B later remarks that the portrait bust by Lorenzo Bartolini makes him look like 'a superannuated Jesuit').

6   B visits the Shelleys.

8   Mary Shelley reads aloud the first two acts of *Werner*.

9   Williams dines with B; their conversation includes B's recollections that *The Corsair* was completed in ten nights, during which he 'lived chiefly upon biscuits and soda water', and that *BA* was written in three days (Williams' journal).

11 Williams calls on B and finds another sitting to Bartolini in progress. Shelley tells Peacock that he and B are 'constant companions'.

12 B thanks Sir Walter Scott for accepting the dedication of *Cain*, and suggests that he visit Italy.

15 B meets Trelawny, who has arrived in Pisa the previous day.

Williams calls on B and they, with other friends, practise pistol-shooting; later they dine at Shelley's home and go to the opera.

16   Bartolini, Trelawny, Williams and others dine with B.

19   Williams calls on B, 'who wishes to have a boat on the model of ours now building at Genoa – intending to enter into a competition with us in sailing' (Williams' journal).

20   B finishes his tragedy *Werner: or, The Inheritance*. On the 22nd he tells Murray that he will send it to Kinnaird to be placed in the hands of some other publisher (his relations with Murray have evidently become strained); on the same day, he sends the manuscript of *H&E* to Kinnaird and instructs him to place it with 'any publisher you please', not excluding Murray, mentioning at the same time that he has another new drama (i.e. *Werner*) ready for publication in the same volume.

22   B's thirty-fourth birthday.

25   Shelley tells Horace Smith that 'Lord Byron unites us at a weekly dinner where my nerves are generally shaken to pieces by sitting up, contemplating the rest making themselves vats of claret &c. till 3 o'Clock in the morning'.

27   Greek independence is proclaimed.

28   Death of Lady Noel, B's mother-in-law. B hears of her death on 15 February (see below).

February

Relations between Shelley and B become strained at about this time: Shelley tells Claire Clairmont (in an undated letter) that he intends to 'put a period to' his intimacy with B, and on 18 June he tells John Gisborne, 'I detest all society – almost all, at least – and Lord Byron is the nucleus of all that is hateful and tiresome in it.'

3   (Sun) Williams calls on B (one of numerous visits, not all noted here, during this period).

5   Writes a long letter to the editor of the *Courier*, which has published a letter from Southey referring to B's attack on him in *TF*; B's letter, which attacks Southey's comments point by point, was never sent and was not published until 1954. He also decides to proceed with publication of *VJ*, in which Southey is held up to ridicule, and on the 6th writes to Kinnaird urging him to find a publisher for the poem or, failing that, to have it privately printed and distributed among friends. On the 7th B writes to Southey, challenging him to a

duel; the letter is not sent at once, but is forwarded on the 23rd to Kinnaird, who fails to send it to Southey.

9   Mary Shelley tells Maria Gisborne that B is having 'a large & beautiful boat' built in Genoa (it is being built under the supervision of Captain Daniel Roberts, who built Shelley's boat, the *Don Juan*).

15 B hears the news of his mother-in-law's death (see 28 Jan); in the ensuing weeks B is heavily involved in business matters relating to her estate, in which he is a substantial legatee.

17 Asks Kinnaird to insure Lady Byron's life on his behalf, so that some provision for his children is made in the case of her death. (From this date to the end of his life B signs himself Noel Byron, Lady Noel's will stipulating that he take the Noel arms.) Shelley tells Hunt that B has 'furnished with *tolerable willingness*' the £250 requested by Hunt to cover the expenses of bringing his family to Italy, and has accepted Shelley's guarantee for the debt; Shelley has evidently found the negotiation with B a painful business.

18 Williams calls on B, 'who talks of getting up *Othello*' (Williams' journal); according to Trelawny's later recollections, B was to play Iago.

20 B and Williams ride together to the shooting-ground and practise pistol-shooting.

23 Writes to Kinnaird concerning the challenge to Southey (see 5 Feb); B is prepared to travel to England if necessary and will fight him 'on the day of my landing', but would prefer to avoid publicity by meeting Southey on the French coast.

28 Williams' journal notes that the plan to perform *Othello* (see the 18th) has now been abandoned.

March

4 (Mon) Tells Moore that he is 'no enemy to religion, but the contrary'.

6 Tells Moore that *Werner* may be sent to Murray, who has evidently made placatory approaches. On the same day B writes to Murray saying that he is prepared to 'make peace' with him. On the 8th he tells Moore that one of the conditions of his reconciliation with Murray is that the latter must publish Taaffe's commentary on Dante.

8 Shelley and Williams dine with B; when Shelley repeats 'some of the finest lines' of *CH*, B exclaims, 'Heavens! Shelley,

what infinite nonsense are you quoting?' (Williams' journal).
15 Tells Murray that he has 'no desire' to revisit England.
24 While B, Shelley and others are riding in the vicinity of Pisa, they are treated rudely by Stefani Masi, a non-commissioned officer, who is stabbed (not fatally) in the ensuing quarrel. Shelley and John Hay suffer minor injuries. The police are informed, depositions are made, and the affair is reported to the British Minister in Florence. B sends an English physician to attend Masi, who soon recovers from his wound. On the 28th, B's servant Tita (Giovanni Falcieri) is arrested. B's coachman, Vincenzo Papi, who was responsible for wounding Masi, is arrested but released. (Williams' journal, excerpted in *I&R*, pp. 84–9, furnishes a detailed account of the episode.) The affair occupies B a good deal during the following month.

April
 9 (Tues) Promises Murray that he will send the busts of himself and Teresa, executed by Bartolini, as soon as they are finished. (On 16 May he tells Murray that they are 'not even begun'; but see 3 Jan.)
12 Tells John Hay that his servant Tita and one of Teresa's servants are being held in prison in spite of their innocence; B is distressed by their plight.
14 Williams calls on B, and finds him beginning canto VI of *DJ*. (Williams' visits during this period are very numerous.)
15 Claire Clairmont arrives in Pisa.
20 Rogers arrives in Pisa and immediately visits B, who on 2 May tells Kinnaird that he treated Rogers 'with all attention in my power – in return for which he will probably abuse me – as he does every body'. Tita is sent into exile (but later rejoins his master). Death of Allegra, aged five, from typhus fever; B hears the news soon afterwards, since he informs Murray of it on the 22nd; on 17 May he tells Moore that the loss has been a 'serious blow' to him. He later arranges for the child's body to be shipped to England for burial (see 26 May). On the 23rd, Claire Clairmont leaves for Spezia with the Williamses in order to look for a house there; they return to Pisa on the 25th, but on the same day Shelley sends her, with Mary Shelley and Trelawny, back to Spezia, and she perhaps does not learn of the child's death until 2 May.
26 Williams, who is leaving for Spezia, calls on B to say goodbye.

In the issue of the *Edinburgh Review* that appears this month (dated Feb), Jeffrey attacks *DJ*.

May

16 (Thurs) Sends a letter of sharp reproof to Murray, who has failed to acknowledge receipt of the poems sent to him via Kinnaird and Moore (but his letter croses with one from Murray).

21 Visits the American squadron, which is lying in Leghorn harbour, and is elaborately entertained. At about this time, B moves to the Villa Dupuy, near Leghorn: the house has 'the islands of Elba and Corsica visible from my balcony, and my old friend the Mediterranean rolling blue at my feet' (to Isaac D'Israeli, 10 June).

26 Tells Murray that Allegra's body is now on its way to England and that he wishes her to be buried at Harrow: He describes in precise detail the spot in the churchyard where he would wish her to lie – 'a favourite spot' of his boyhood, where he 'used to sit for hours & hours' – but concludes that she had better be buried in the church, where he will erect a tablet to her memory. He gives directions for the inscription and the funeral service.

June

Early in the month B receives a brief visit from Lord Clare, 'my earliest and dearest friend' (to Moore, 8 June).

2 (Sun) Leigh Hunt reviews *Cain* in the *Examiner*. Mary Shelley writes to Maria Gisborne concerning Allegra's death: 'Lord Byron felt the loss at first bitterly; he also felt remorse, for he felt that he had acted against everybody's counsels and wishes . . . .'

6 Returns to Murray the corrected proofs of part of *Werner*, and tells him that he is sending the *Detached Thoughts*, to be used in conjunction with the memoirs for posthumous publication.

12 In a letter to Edward Ellice, B revives his earlier notions (originating in 1819) of emigration to South America: he specifically refers to a project to sail to Angostura in Venezuela ('Bolivar's country'), and asks for information concerning the present state of the country (see also 16 Aug).

18 B's yacht the *Bolivar*, 'a little thing of about 22 tons' (to Edward Dawkins, 26 June), arrives in Leghorn from Genoa, having been brought thither by Trelawny.

July

Work on *DJ* is resumed during this month, and by the 24th B has 'nearly completed three more Cantos' (to Kinnaird).

4   (Thurs) Shelley writes to his wife, 'Lord Byron is at this moment on the point of leaving Tuscany. The Gambas have been exiled, and he declares his intention of following their fortunes. His first idea was to sail to America, which has been changed to Switzerland, then to Genoa, and last to Lucca.'

8   Tells Murray that he will contribute to a periodical that Hunt is thinking of establishing. (Hunt has arrived with his family in Pisa at the beginning of the month and settled at the Casa Lanfranchi, where B and Teresa are also now living.) On the same day Hunt writes to a correspondent that B is entering 'with great ardour' into plans for the new periodical, still at this stage named *Hesperides*. On the 12th, B tells Moore that *VJ* will probably appear in the first number of the new periodical (as it does, on 15 Oct). B asks Moore to send a contribution to Hunt, but makes it clear that he does not share Hunt's optimism about its chances of success (in the event, only four issues appear). On the 8th, Shelley and Williams set off from Leghorn in their boat the *Don Juan*, intending to sail to Lerici; both are drowned when the boat presumably founders during a storm in the Bay of Spezia. According to Moore's later account, B had a premonition of disaster about ten days before Shelley's death (see *I&R*, p. 98). Trelawny, according to his own later account, informs B that Shelley is missing on the 11th.

16 Shelley's body is washed ashore: it is in an advanced state of decomposition and is much battered, but a copy of Keats's 1820 *Poems* in the pocket enables it to be identified. Williams' body is found on the 18th, and both are promptly buried on the beach in accordance with local health regulations. Williams' body is exhumed and cremated on 15 August and Shelley's on 16 August. B makes two journeys 'to the mouth of the Arno' (to Kinnaird, 19 July) on the 17th and 18th July 'for the purpose of ascertaining the circumstances and identifications of the bodies', but is too late to witness the interment; he is, however, present for Shelley's cremation on 16 August. B is named in Shelley's will as one of his executors, but later declines to act and also refuses a legacy of £2000.

August

8 (Thurs) Tells Moore that he has not seen the hostile publication *Memoirs of the Life and Writings of the Right Honourable Lord Byron* (anonymous, but by John Watkins), and has no wish to do so. He has finished three more cantos (VI–VIII) of *DJ* and is 'hovering on the brink of another'.

16 With Hunt and Trelawny, B attends the cremation of Shelley's remains on the beach at Viareggio. Trelawny's numerous accounts of the scene, and of B's remarks on the occasion, are graphic but unreliable. While the cremation is in progress, B swims out to the *Bolivar* and back (a distance of three miles or more) at midday; as a result, he suffers a 'feverish attack' (to Moore, 27 Aug) and severe sunburning. Trelawny later states that B 'wished much to have the skull [of Shelley] if possible' but that it disintegrated. Shelley's heart, unconsumed by the fire, is given by Trelawny to Hunt, who subsequently refuses to give it to Mary Shelley when she asks for it; Mary asks for B's assistance, but the matter is eventually resolved by the intervention of Mrs Williams. Writing to Moore on the 16th, B states that he is now 'fluctuating' between South America and Greece (see 12 June and 23–4 Sept).

24 Tells Kinnaird that he has written 'nearly *four*' cantos of *DJ* – that is, the ninth is near completion.

?27 Mary Shelley tells Maria Gisborne that B 'comes to see us about once a week, accompanied by the Guiccioli'.

31 Archibald Murray, half-brother of John Murray, calls on B.

September

2 (Mon) Tells Hobhouse that he is packing for removal to Genoa, where he has taken a house for a year.

7 Sends Kinnaird the sixth and seventh cantos of *DJ*, and promises that the eighth and ninth will follow shortly (as they do on 10 Sep).

15 Hobhouse arrives in Pisa, calls on B, and finds him 'much changed – his face fatter, and the expression of it injured'. Hobhouse spends the evening with B and does so again on the 17th and 18th.

18 B sends Kinnaird three sarcastic epitaphs on Castlereagh, who has committed suicide on 12 August. Captain Daniel Roberts consults B about defraying the expenses of salvaging Shelley's boat.

19 Hobhouse goes riding with B.
20 A storm prevents Hobhouse and B from riding together again, so Hobhouse sits at home with B, who 'talks of coming to England in the spring'.
23 B tells Kinnaird that he has 'some flying notions of emigration'. He informs Bartolini that he requires delivery of the two busts, 'finished or unfinished'.
24 Tells Kinnaird that he has for a long time had 'a notion of emigration from your worn out Europe . . . [to] South America – The United States – or even van Diemen's Land'.
27 Leaves Pisa for Genoa.

October
?3 (Thurs) Arrives at Albaro and settles at the Casa Saluzzo, 'on a hill overlooking Genoa' (to Hoppner, 2 Jan 1823). Teresa and her father and brother live in the same house; Mary Shelley and Leigh Hunt, his wife and six children (see next entry) eventually establish themselves in another house in the neighbourhood.
 4 Tells Mary Shelley that he was ill and confined to bed for four days at Lerici during the journey to Genoa; also that Leigh Hunt and his family ('six little blackguards') are making their way from Pisa to join him in Genoa.
 9 Tells Murray that canto x of *DJ* is finished but not yet copied, and canto xɪ has been begun. He also complains that John Hunt (brother of Leigh Hunt) has advertised him as a contributor to *The Liberal*.
15 The first number of *The Liberal*, which includes *VJ*, appears.
19 Mary Shelley sees B for the first time for 'about a month': she spends two hours with him and afterwards writes that, in B's company, 'I can never cease for a second to have [Shelley] in my heart and brain with a clearness that mocks reality'.
20 Offers to pay the travelling-expenses of Augusta and her husband and family if she will settle in Nice; he urges the wisdom of the move from the point of view of economy, and adds that he would be prepared, if she agreed, to move to Nice himself so as to be near her.
22 Reproaches Murray in strong terms for failing to give John Hunt B's preface to *VJ* along with the poem, which has been published (see the 15th) without the preface.
24 Another and longer letter to Murray contains a catalogue of

reproaches; but the postscript, added after the receipt of a letter from Murray, is couched in more forgiving terms.

27 Tells Kinnaird that he has been suffering from a cough and has lost weight.

31 Tells John Hunt that he is taking all his completed and unpublished poems out of Murray's hands. He offers *Werner* and *H&E* to Hunt for publication in *The Liberal*. (See 23 Nov.)

November

6   (Wed) Writes to Murray in even stronger terms, telling him, 'As a publisher I bid you a final farewell' (the letter was never received but was retained by Kinnaird).

14 Sends Mary Shelley part of *The Deformed Transformed* to be copied – a service she often performs for him.

18 Writes to Murray modifying some of his earlier complaints.

23 *Werner* is publihed by Murray.

During this month James (now Sir James) Wedderburn Webster and Lady Hardy visit B in Genoa. On 1 December B tells Kinnaird that Webster, who had not seen him for about ten years, found him looking thinner; he adds that he is compelled to diet 'on medical advice'. He also recalls, with some bitterness, that Webster shows no sign of repaying the loan of £1000 made by B ten years earlier, or even the interest upon it that has accrued.

December

9   (Mon) Tells Kinnaird that he has completed canto xii of *DJ*.

14 Tells Hobhouse that he has been unwell from time to time ever since 'that stupid long swim' on 16 August.

14 Sends canto xii of *DJ* to Kinnaird.

16 Tells Kinnaird that he is 'living very economically' and has saved £3300 out of the year's income, even though he has spent £1000 on his schooner and has given more than £300 to Leigh Hunt.

19 Tells Kinnaird that he has been 'not very well' for some time and has seen an English physician; again, he traces the source of his troubles to the reckless swim on 16 August.

23 Reminds Kinnaird that he now has seven unpublished cantos of *DJ* in his hands, and asks him to explore the possibility of their being published by John Hunt in two volumes.

25 Tells Murray that he is thinking of visiting Naples in the spring and of writing a fifth and sixth canto of *CH* (but see 24 Feb 1823); also that 'No Girl will ever be seduced' by reading *DJ*.

1823

January
1 (Wed) *H&E* appears in the second number of *The Liberal*.
2 Tells Hoppner that he has been 'very unwell' but is now better.
7 Writes to Shelley's father to plead the case of his widow and child, who are 'totally destitute' (Mary Shelley is still living near B, lacking the money to return to England).
10 *The Age of Bronze* is finished, and is being copied by Mary Shelley, by this date.
12 Tells Webster that he is 'tormented with chilblains' and hardly able to move.
16 Tells Kinnaird that he is thinking of 'going to Greece perhaps to America', and sends him the corrected proofs of canto VI of *DJ* and the manuscript of *AB*.
18 Tells Kinnaird, by way of explanation of his concern with 'accumulation and retrenchment' in his financial affairs, that his 'most extravagant passions have pretty well subsided', and that the ostentatious extravagance of his youth is now a thing of the past.
22 B's thirty-fifth birthday.
25 Tells Leigh Hunt that he is at work on *The Island*.

February
1 (Sat) Sends Kinnaird an additional passage for insertion in *AB*.
6 Sends the corrected proofs of canto VII of *DJ* to Kinnaird.
10 Tells Webster that he is unable to lend him money.
20 Sends the corrected proofs of canto VIII of *DJ* to Kinnaird.
24 Tells Kinnaird that he has decided not to go to Naples or to continue *CH* (it later emerges that Murray has spread a rumour that a continuation may be expected); also that canto XIII of *DJ* was completed 'the other day'.
27 Tells Kinnaird that he awaits proofs of cantos IX–XII of *DJ* but

does not wish to see a proof of *AB*; he does nevertheless see and correct a proof of the latter early in March. Tells Hoppner that he is 'far from well' and 'as thin as a Skeleton'.

28 Mary Shelley tells a correspondent that B has offered 'to provide means for my return to England'.

During this month B tries in vain to effect a reconciliation between Webster and his wife, who have separated.

March

3 (Mon) Promises Kinnaird that he will shortly send him cantos XIII and XIV of *DJ*.

5 In a letter to B. W. Procter ('Barry Cornwall'), B describes *DJ* as 'a satire on affectations of all kinds, mixed with some relief of serious feeling and description'.

8 Tells Kinnaird that canto XIII of *DJ* has been sent and canto XIV is being copied. He also sends the manuscript of *The Island*.

10 Sends canto XIV of *DJ* to Kinnaird.

15 Dines with William Hill, the British Minister at Genoa; on the way home, B's carriage breaks down and he walks three miles in a cold wind; as a result he catches a severe chill.

17 Tells John Hunt that he is eager to read Scott's *Peveril of the Peak*.

20 Tells Kinnaird that canto XV of *DJ* is nearly finished; it is sent to Kinnaird on the 31st.

31 Receives a visit from Henry Fox, son of Lord Holland.

April

1 (Tues) *AB* is published by John Hunt. B meets Marguerite, Countess of Blessington, who, with her husband, her sister (Mary Power) and Alfred, Count D'Orsay, has arrived in Genoa the previous day. For her first impressions of B, whom she was eager to meet, see *I&R*, pp. 28–9. During the next two months, B and the Blessingtons meet frequently.

5 Tells Edward Blaquière that he will be 'delighted' to see him and Andreas Luriottis (they are on the way to Greece: Luriottis has visited England on behalf of the Greek government in order to try to enlist support for the Greek uprising against the Turks, and Blaquière is a member of the London Greek Committee who is visiting Greece to investigate the state of affairs there on behalf of the Committee). B evidently sees them later on the same day, expresses his sympathy with their cause, offers his

services, and expresses his willingness to visit Greece in July. Blaquière invites him to become a member of the Committee. (B predicts to Hobhouse on 7 Apr that Teresa will be unwilling to see him go, but notes that her brother, Pietro Gamba, will be eager to join him.) B returns Count D'Orsay's journal, which he has perused with interest and praises highly.

9   Tells Kinnaird that it is 'probable' that he may go to Greece.

12   Lady Blessington rides with B (and again on the 16th and 17th).

14   Tells John Hunt that he has printed too many copies (2000) of *AB*, and that canto xvi of *DJ* is 'nearly finished'. (His concern about *AB* proves unfounded, since in the event about 2000 copies seem to have been sold during the first week: see B to Kinnaird, 21 Apr.)

19   Tells Kinnaird that there is 'some risk of not returning' if he goes to Greece.

22   Takes Lady Blessington to see the Lomelini Gardens.

29   Notes in a letter to John Hunt that the sales of *AB* are proof of 'a decline of popularity to a great extent' when compared with those of some of his earlier works, notably *Corsair*. Rides with Lady Blessington.

30   Drinks tea with the Blessingtons.

May

During this period B continues to return corrected proofs of *DJ* at intervals to Kinnaird.

1   (Thurs) Rides with Lady Blessington and Pietro Gamba.

4   Rides with Lady Blessington and afterwards dines with the Blessingtons.

5   Thanks Edward Le Mesurier, a retired English naval lieutenant settled in Italy, for the gift of a Newfoundland dog ('Lyon'). It later accompanies him to Greece and is taken to England with his body.

6   Finishes canto xvi of *DJ*, which is sent to Kinnaird soon afterwards.

10   B 'talks [to Lady Blessington] of going to Greece, and made many jests of his intention of turning soldier' (Lady Blessington, *Conversations*).

12   Acknowledges a letter from the London Greek Committee, who have informed him that he has been appointed a member of the Committee. B states that he intends to go to Greece 'in person' and will try to surmount the only obstacle

standing in his path, which is 'of a domestic nature' (i.e. Teresa's objections).

13 Dines with the Blessingtons.

16 Rides with Lady Blessington, who records that he is 'in low spirits' and 'speaks with great bitterness . . . of the treatment he experienced in England'.

21 Tells Kinnaird that he is 'doing all I can to get away', but that Teresa is proving difficult; on the same day he tells Captain Roberts that it is 'more than probable' that he will go to Greece.

28 Sends corrected proof of canto xv of *DJ* to Kinnaird.

29 Dines with the Blessingtons.

During this and the next month, B sells his schooner *Bolivar* to Lord Blessington and purchases from Lady Blessington an Arabian horse, Mameluke, to take to Greece with him. He is much involved with preparations for the expedition to Greece, including the purchase of arms and medical supplies.

June

1 (Sun) B visits the Blessingtons, who leave Genoa the next day.

15 Tells Trelawny, 'I am at last determined to go to Greece; it is the only place I was ever contented in', and invites Trelawny to accompany him.

19 Tells Hobhouse and Kinnaird that he has engaged a brig (the *Hercules*), and expects to sail for Greece early in July.

28 Tells Leigh Hunt that Mary Shelley has declined to receive financial assistance from B to enable her to return to England; he offers to advance the money to Hunt, who can then give it to her as if it were a loan obtained from another source. (Mary Shelley's letter of a slightly later date to Jane Williams states that B conveyed to Hunt 'such an air of unwillingness and sense of the obligation he conferred' that Hunt reminded her that B owed her £1000. For the origin of this debt, see 25 Dec 1821.)

July

12 (Sat) B has set this as the date for his departure, but light and unfavourable winds make it impossible.

13 B and his party, which includes Count Pietro Gamba, Trelawny, and Dr Francesco Bruno (whom B has engaged as

his personal physician) go on board the *Hercules*, commanded
by Captain John Scott. The ship is still becalmed, however,
and they go ashore again the next day.

15 They set sail but soon encounter a storm that drives them
back to Genoa.

16 They set off again, and on the 22nd arrive in Leghorn.

22 Writing from Leghorn, B thanks Goethe for some lines sent
to him in response to his own letter expressing his admiration
for the German writer. At Leghorn, James Hamilton Browne
joins B's party.

23 Trelawny writes to Captain Roberts that B and himself are
'extraordinarily thick, we are inseparable'.

August

3 (Sun) The *Hercules* arrives at Argostoli, on the island of
Cephalonia. B finds that Blaquière has left for England, and
that Greek affairs are in a state of confusion. He explores the
area ('a tour over the hills here in our old style': to Hobhouse,
11 Sep), and in the middle of the month (11th–17th) visits
Ithaca. On the evening of the 17th he returns to the *Hercules*
'in admirable spirits' (according to Browne).

September

4 (Thurs) Moves to Metaxata in south-west Cephalonia: 'a very
pretty village . . . between the mountains and the Sea' (to
Augusta, 12 Oct).

6 Browne and Trelawny set off for the Morea.

28 B begins his Cephalonia journal by summarising his
experiences since leaving Genoa; he continues it on the 30th,
but breaks off after receiving news from Augusta that Ada is
ill, which causes him great concern. Early in November he
receives news of her recovery, but only resumes the journal
on 17 December.

October

Early in the month there are earthquakes in Cephalonia; they
recur later in the month.

10 (Fri) Rides and dines with Dr Henry Muir, health officer at
Argostoli.

12 Writes to Augusta making enquiries about Ada's appearance
and character.

28 Lord Sydney Osborne arrives in Metaxata and meets B: they
    have lunch together, and on the following day meet again as
    dinner guests of Colonel Charles Napier, commander of the
    British garrison on Cephalonia and a sympathiser with the
    Greek cause, who had first met B in August.
During this month B also receives a visit from George Finlay, a
young Scot (and later a distinguished historian) who has come
out to take part in the Greek struggle.

November
12 (Wed) Draws bills on his London bankers for £4000 'in favour
    of the Greek Provisional Government to enable part of their
    fleet to succour Messolonghi now in a state of blockade' (to
    David Grant).
29 Tells Teresa that he is very busy seeing people from various
    nations who have an interest in the Greek cause – 'all with
    something to say to me'. Colonel Leicester Stanhope, son of
    the Earl of Harrington, who has been appointed an agent of
    the Greek Committee in London on 21 September, arrives on
    22 November; earlier in the month Browne returns from the
    Morea, accompanied by Andreas Luriottis and Jean Orlando,
    representatives of the Greek government; during the month
    Dr Julius Millingen, who has been sent out by the Greek
    Committee to provide medical aid for the Greeks, and who is
    to attend B during his last days, also arrives.

December
 2 (Tues) Tells Prince Alexander Mavrocordatos, Greek patriot
    and leader, who later becomes Prime Minister of Greece, that
    his country must now choose whether to win her freedom or
    to become a province of Turkey or a colony of a European
    power: 'never again will she have the chance, never again'.
 6 Stanhope sets off for Missolonghi, as Millingen also does two
    days later.
14 Tells Teresa that he and her brother are 'occupied all day and
    every day with Greek business'.
17 Resumes, briefly, his journal; then abandons it again until 15
    February.
23 Tells Kinnaird that he expects to embark at any moment for
    Missolonghi (Mavrocordatos has arrived there and assumed
    command on the 11th). Tells Charles Barry, his banker in

Genoa, that he has no intention of returning but will 'see this Greek business out (or *it me*)'.

27   Tells Moore that he is leaving for Missolonghi the next day; in fact he embarks on the 29th, arrives in Zante the next morning, and sails for Missolonghi the same evening. When Dr James Kennedy visits him to say farewell on the 29th, he finds him reading Scott's *Quentin Durward*.

31   B's boat is chased by a Turkish vessel but escapes; Count Pietro Gamba, however, who is in another boat, is captured, together with servants, horses and money belonging to B, and carried into Patras.

1824

January

3   (Sat) B arrives in Misslonghi after an adventurous journey during which, after fleeing from the Turks (see 31ᵗ Dec 1823), B's boat is chased 'from Creek to Creek – as far as Dragomestri', is 'twice driven on the rocks', and narrowly escapes shipwreck (to Lord Sydney Osborne, 7 Jan). The other boat, in which Count Pietro Gamba is travelling, having been released by the Turks, arrives in Missolonghi on the same day as B.

4   B disembarks and receives an enthusiastic welcome.

13   Tells Charles Hancock that he is thinking of undertaking an expedition shortly.

15   John Hunt stands trial for publishing *VJ* in *The Liberal* and is found guilty; sentence is not passed until 19 July, when he is fined £100 and required 'to enter into securities [for £2000] for five years'.

19   B tells G. Stevens that he is 'preparing for active operations' and intends to 'stick by the Greeks to the last rag of canvas or shirt'. At about this time he undertakes to accept into his service for a year, and to be responsible for paying, 500 Suliotes.

22   B's thirty-sixth birthday: he composes 'On This Day I Complete my Thirty-Sixth Year'.

28   Tells John Bowring that they are blockaded by a Turkish squadron of sixteen vessels and that plans are afoot for an

expedition of some 2000 soldiers to attack Lepanto (on the 25th Mavrocordatos has asked B to lead this expedition).

31   Mavrocordatos visits B.

February

7   (Sat) Major William Parry, an artillery expert dispatched by the Greek Committee in London, meets B and sees him frequently thereafter.

15   In the evening, according to Parry, after complaining of thirst, B drinks a glass of cider and then collapses, loses consciousness, and falls into convulsions, but with medical assistance soon recovers. According to Millingen's account, B has previously drunk a large amount of punch in the company of Parry, who is a heavy drinker; Millingen describes B's symptoms as resembling those of an epileptic fit.

17   B resumes his journal briefly, to recount that on the 15th he was seized by 'a strong shock of a Convulsive description' lasting about ten minutes, the nature of which has not been determined by his doctors. After his time, according to Gamba, B 'lived with the strictest abstinence: vegetables and a little fish were his only food. But he took too much medicine, as indeed he was accustomed at all times to do.'

21   Severe earthquake at Missolonghi. Though weak, B is now 'a good deal better' (to Samuel Barff). He has secured the release of 28 Turkish prisoners, mainly women and children, and has sent them at his own expense to Prevesa for repatriation. He has thoughts of adopting a ten-year-old Turkish girl, and suggests to Augusta on the 23rd that she might be received by Lady Byron as a companion for Ada (the scheme is not pursued).

March

4   (Thurs) Receives a visit from Mavrocordatos.

13   Tells Kinnaird that the plague has broken out in Missolonghi.

18   A message arrives from Colonel Stanhope, who has left for Athens on 21 February and is now there, inviting B and Mavrocordatos to a conference to be held at Salona; however, unfavourable weather and impassable roads prevent their setting off. At this time, according to Gamba's later recollections, B has 'become very thin', his temper is 'irritable', and he often complains of 'not feeling well, of vertigos in the

head, of a disposition to faint, and occasionally he told me
that he experienced a sort of alarm without any apparent
cause'.

19 B tells Bowring that preparations are going ahead for 'the
ensuing campaign'.

April

 9 (Fri) B writes his last surviving letters. According to Gamba,
he receives letters from England, including encouraging news
of Ada's health and a silhouette profile of her. He goes
riding, but is 'caught in a heavy rain' and becomes soaked.
After his return he quickly develops feverish and rheumatic
symptoms and is in considerable pain; he refuses, however,
to allow his physicians to bleed him (according to Millingen's
later account, 'the patient entertained a deep-rooted prejudice
against bleeding').

10 The fever continues, but B is up and conducts business.

11 He goes for a long ride and seems 'in better health and
spirits' (Gamba). (According to Fletcher's and Millingen's
accounts, however, this last ride takes place on the 10th.)

12 B remains in bed 'with a rheumatic fever' (Gamba).

13 He rises but does not leave the house: 'His fever was allayed,
but his pains still continued. He was out of spirits and
irritable' (Gamba).

14 Rises at noon but is weak; his doctors discourage him from
riding.

15 His condition seems to improve, though the fever continues
and he is unable to sleep.

17 He talks to Gamba 'in a sepulchral tone', and seems to him
'too calm'. According to Fletcher's later account, the doctors
now bleed B for the first time, and twice more in the course
of the day; Gamba states that he was bled twice on this day,
losing 'about two pounds of blood'; Millingen's account states
that 'about twenty ounces' of blood were taken on the 16th
and that he was bled twice more on the 17th. During the
night of the 17th/18th he is delirious.

18 Easter Sunday. B refuses to be bled (according to Gamba,
'About this time Dr Bruno entreated him, with tears in his
eyes, to be again bled. "No," he said: "if my hour is come, I
shall die whether I lose my blood or keep it."'). He is made
aware of the seriousness of his condition. Dr Thomas, an

English physician who practises on the island of Zante (about fifty miles from Missolonghi) is sent for.

At about 6 p.m. he falls asleep and never regains consciousness. There are various accounts of his last words, including two different versions by Fletcher (see *I&R*, pp. 158–9, and compare Millingen's account given on p. 164).

19   B dies at about 6 p.m. According to Millingen, one of his last requests was: 'Let not my body be hacked, or be sent to England. Here let my bones moulder. – Lay me in the first corner without pomp or nonsense.' Despite this, Gamba urges that 'a great man belonged to his country' (Millingen), and after an autopsy has been performed the body is embalmed by the doctors. The lungs are removed and placed in an urn which is put in the church at Missolonghi (from where they subsequently disappear). The other internal organs, contained in four jars, are shipped back to England with the body. (According to Blaquière's account, the heart was taken to the church 'in procession' on the 24th: perhaps 'heart' is a slip for 'lungs'.)

30   B's remains are conveyed on board the *Florida*, bound for England: 'The coffin was carried down to the sea side, on the shoulders of four military Chiefs, and attended in the same order as before; minute guns continued to be discharged till the moment of embarkation; these were followed by a salute of thirty-seven cannon' (Blaquière; B was, of course, in his thirty-seventh year when he died).

May
14   (Fri) Kinnaird, in London, receives news of B's death, and immediately communicates with Hobhouse. The news circulates rapidly, for on the same day Moore learns of B's death and at once asks Murray 'when it will be convenient to you to complete the arrangement with respect to the Memoirs which we agreed upon'.

17   B's memoirs are burned in Murray's office in Albemarle Street; Murray, Moore, Hobhouse and other witnesses are present.

June
19   (Sat) Hobhouse and Hanson deposit B's will at Doctors' Commons: 'By a curious coincidence, Hanson told me that

the room in which we delivered in the will was the very one to which he accompanied Lord Byron when my friend applied for his marriage licence' (Hobhouse).

July

1 (Thurs) Hobhouse hears that the *Florida* is in the Downs, and he proceeds to Rochester. The next day he boards the vessel, which anchors at Gravesend, later proceeding to London docks.

5 Hobhouse declines an invitation to view the body, which he is assured by an undertaker has 'almost all the freshness and firmness of life'. (When he plucks up courage the next day and sees it, 'It did not bear the slightest resemblance to my dear friend.') The coffin and the box containing the heart are conveyed by barge to Palace Yard Stairs, the river banks being 'crowded with spectators', and are taken to the front parlour of Sir Edward Knatchbull's house in Great George Street, Westminster, where a room 'decently hung with black', with 'no other decoration than an escutcheon of the Byron arms, roughly daubed on a deal board' (Hobhouse), has been prepared. Augusta has indicated that it is the wish of the family that B should be buried in the family vault at Hucknall, Nottinghamshire. B's coffin lies in state (the phrase is used by Hobhouse) on the 9th and 10th, and is visited by members of 'the nobility and gentry' (*The Times*, 10 July), admission being by ticket.

12 At 9 a.m. the funeral cortège leaves the house and proceeds north. According to Hobhouse, 'about 47 carriages', many of them empty, follow the body through the London streets; *The Times* the next day lists four mourning-coaches and nearly forty carriages, referring also to 'many others'. Hobhouse, as executor, supervises the proceedings. Moore, who records the occasion in his journal, travels in one of the mourning-coaches together with Rogers, Campbell, Stanhope and Orlando. Once beyond the city limits, the hearse proceeds north; overnight stops are made at Welwyn, Hertfordshire (12th); Higham Ferrers, Northamptonshire (13th); and Oakham, Rutland (14th). The body arrives in Nottingham on the 15th, and burial in the family vault at Hucknall Torkard takes place on the 16th. According to Hobhouse, a large crowd congregates and the funeral procession, which includes

the Mayor and Corporation of Nottingham, is about a quarter of a mile long and, 'moving very slowly, was five hours on the road to Hucknall'. The church and churchyard are crowded 'until a late hour in the evening', and the vault is not closed until the next morning.

The flow of biographies, memoirs and reminiscences is in full spate within a short time after B's death. The more significant items are listed in the bibliography below. On 5 November 1824 Moore tells a correspondent that 'It was always Lord Byron's wish' that he should be his biographer, and that he plans to produce a life, for which he solicits materials, 'in the course of the following year'. On 21 December 1825 he asks Hobhouse whether he would be willing to join him in the work; Hobhouse declines. Moore's book is not published until 1830–1.

Of those of Byron's family and friends who outlived him, Augusta died in 1851 and Lady Byron in 1860. Ada married Lord King (created Earl of Lovelace in 1838) in 1835, and died in 1852. Caroline Lamb died in 1828; Kinnaird in 1830; Murray in 1843; Mary Shelley in 1851; Hodgson and Moore in 1852; Leigh Hunt in 1859; Hobhouse and Medwin in 1869; Hoppner in 1872; Claire Clairmont and Teresa Guiccioli in 1879; and Trelawny in 1881.

The Byron Circle

'Circle' is used here as an elastic term, and includes not only members of Byron's family and his close friends but more casual acquaintances whose names appear in the foregoing chronology. Those whose appearances are of merely passing interest have, however, been omitted.

Baillie, Joanna (1762–1851), Scottish poet and dramatist, and a friend of Sir Walter Scott.

Bankes, William (died 1856), a friend of Byron's at Trinity College, Cambridge. In a letter of 19 November 1820, Byron recalled that at Trinity Bankes had been 'the father of all mischiefs'.

Blaquière, Edward, one of the founders of the Greek Committee in London, met Byron in Genoa in April 1823; at the time Blaquière was on his way to Greece to investigate the situation there. They met again in Greece, and Blaquière's *Narrative of a Second Visit to Greece* (1825) includes an account of Byron's last days.

Blessington, Marguerite, Countess of (1789–1849), the second wife of Lord Blessington, whom Byron had known slightly in London. Arriving in Genoa in the course of a Continental tour at the end of March 1823, she wrote in her diary, 'Desirous as I am to see "Genoa the Superb", . . . I confess that its being the residence of Lord Byron gives it a still greater attraction for me.' She saw much of Byron during the ensuing two months, and on the basis of her notes made during this period she later produced her *Conversations of Lord Byron*, serialised in the *New Monthly Magazine* in 1832–3, published in volume form in 1834, and a great popular success. See Michael Sadleir, *Blessington–D'Orsay: A Masquerade* (1933).

Browne, James Hamilton, a Scot who sympathised with the cause of Greek Independence, was secretary to General Maitland in Corfu and assisted with the negotiation of a loan from Britain to the Greeks. He joined Byron's expedition, meeting him in

Leghorn in July 1823 and travelling to Greece with him. His 'Voyage from Leghorn to Cephalonia with Lord Byron, and a Narrative of a Visit, in 1823, to the Seat of War in Greece', published in *Blackwood's Magazine* in January 1824, contains an account of the journey.

Bruno, Francesco, a young and inexperienced physician (Trelawny dismissed him as 'an unfledged medical student') who accompanied Byron to Greece as his medical adviser and remained with him until his death.

Byron, Lady (Annabella, née Milbanke) (1792–1860), daughter of Sir Ralph and Lady Judith Milbanke of Seaham, County Durham, and a niece of Lady Melbourne. Brought up quietly and educated privately, she developed strong intellectual and literary interests. She met Byron in London, at Lady Melbourne's, on 25 March 1812, when he was basking in the success of *Childe Harold*. She refused his first proposal on 13 September 1812, but accepted his second two years later, and they were married on 2 January 1815. Their daughter Augusta Ada was born on 10 December 1815. On 15 January 1816, Annabella returned to her parents' home and never lived with Byron again. Marchand comments that her later years were 'devoted to "good works" and to self-justification' (*L&J*, II, 284). Byron corresponded with her occasionally during his later years, chiefly concerning the child. Byron's marriage has provoked an extensive literature, including Harriet Beecher Stowe, *Lady Byron Vindicated* (Boston, Mass., 1870); Ralph Milbanke, Earl of Lovelace, *Astarte* (1921); Ethel Colburn Mayne, *The Life and Letters of Anne Isabella, Lady Noel Byron* (1929); G. Wilson Knight, *Lord Byron's Marriage* (1957); Malcolm Elwin, *Lord Byron's Wife* (1962).

Byron, Augusta (1784–1851), daughter of Byron's father by his first wife, and hence Byron's half-sister. Her mother died two days after her birth and she was brought up first by a grandmother and then by an assortment of relatives. She and Byron did not meet during his childhood; they seem to have met for the first time during his Harrow schooldays, and they corresponded from 1804. In 1807 she married a cousin, Colonel George Leigh, and bore him a large family. When she and Byron met again in London in 1813, they fell in love. Byron often visited her at her home near Newmarket. She encouraged him to marry, and later befriended his wife; but at the time of the separation, Byron's relationship with his half-sister became a matter of common gossip. See Peter Gunn, *My Dearest Augusta* (New York, 1968).

Byron, Catherine (1765–1811), mother of Byron, belonged to an old Scottish family and married Captain John Byron in 1785. Leslie Marchand has argued (*L&J*, I, 274) that the usual view of her as unstable and over-indulgent is unjust and relies too exclusively on Byron's own statements, and that her own letters reveal her as 'a woman of warm sympathies and good feeling, abundant good sense, and real love and admiration for her son'. There seems to be no doubt, however, about her violent temper. Byron's relationship with her was stormy during her last years, but her sudden death came as a great shock to him.

Clairmont, Claire (1798–1879) (her name is sometimes given as Clare or Clara; she was in fact originally Mary Jane), daughter of Mary Clairmont, who subsequently became the second wife of William Godwin, political writer; Claire was thus a step-sister of Mary Godwin, his daughter by his first wife (Mary Wollstonecraft), who later married Shelley and was an important member of Byron's circle. Claire threw herself in Byron's way early in 1816 and, after he left England, followed him to Geneva. After she returned to England she bore Byron's child, named Allegra, in Bath on 12 January 1817. The child died in 1822 in the convent where Byron had placed her, against Claire's wishes, to be educated. Claire died unmarried and is commemorated in Henry James's *The Aspern Papers*. See also R. Glyn Grylls, *Claire Clairmont* (1939) and Iris Origo, *Allegra* (1935).

Campbell, Thomas (1777–1844), poet, was very popular during his lifetime. He was present at Rogers' house in November 1811 when Rogers and Moore met Byron for the first time.

Dallas, Robert Charles (1754–1824), man of letters, met Byron in January 1808 and acted as an agent on his behalf in his dealings with publishers. He saw a good deal of Byron during the latter's London years, but his flattery at times aroused Byron's contempt. He later published *Recollections of the Life of Lord Byron, 1808–14* (1824).

Davies, Scrope Berdmore (1783–1852), dandy and gambler, educated at Eton and King's College, Cambridge, of which he became a Fellow in 1805. He was a close associate of Byron during his London years, and visited him at Newstead. Byron, who visited Davies at Cambridge in 1811, describes him in his *Detached Thoughts* as 'one of the cleverest men I ever knew, in conversation'. He lent Byron a considerable sum (borrowed from money-lenders) before Byron left England in July 1809; the debt was repaid in 1814. When Byron left England for good in 1816, Davies accompanied him as far as Dover. He himself fled to the Continent to escape his creditors in 1819. See T. A. J. Burnett, *The Rise and Fall of a Regency Dandy: The Life and Times of Scrope Berdmore Davies* (1981).

Fletcher, William, Byron's valet from 1808 until his death. Not infrequently dismissed, he was always taken back; and Byron's letters contain many references both to Fletcher's shortcomings and to the tribulations he suffered during Byron's travels. He was with Byron when he died, and when Trelawny reached Missolonghi a few days later he found Fletcher alone in the house with the corpse. Blaquière's *Narrative of a Second Visit to Greece* contains Fletcher's recollections (presumably ghosted) of Byron; his account there of Byron's last words may be compared with that given by Fletcher in a letter to Augusta Leigh written on 20 April 1824 (the day after Byron's death) and quoted in Ernest J. Lovell Jr's *His Very Self and Voice*, pp. 648–9.

Frere, John Hookham (1769–1846), poet, parodist, politician, and one of the founders of the *Quarterly Review* as well as a literary adviser to John Murray. He published a mock epic in 1817, written in ottava rima and in conversational style, which provided Byron with a model for his *Beppo* and *Don Juan*.

Galt, John (1779–1839), Scottish novelist. He and Byron met occasionally, on the Continent and in London, between August 1809 and December 1813, and Galt later published a *Life of Lord Byron* (1830).

Gamba, family name of Teresa Guiccioli (see below). Teresa's brother Pietro was an enthusiastic patriot and revolutionary; he met Byron in Ravenna in July 1820 and later accompanied him to

Greece. His relationship with Byron was close and affectionate, and he followed Byron's body to England. Gamba himself died in Greece (of typhoid) in 1827. His *Narrative of Lord Byron's Last Journey to Greece* (1825) contains an interesting account of the final stages of Byron's life.

Gifford, William (1756–1826), first editor of the *Quarterly Review* and literary adviser to John Murray, was also a verse-satirist to whose work Byron was indebted in his *English Bards and Scotch Reviewers*.

Guiccioli, Countess Teresa (?1799–1879), daughter of Count Gamba of Ravenna, was educated at a convent school and at the age of about nineteen married the rich and elderly Count Guiccioli. She met Byron in 1818, and they became lovers in the following year. A decree of separation was granted by the Pope in 1820, and she and Byron lived happily together until his departure for Greece (though it has been suggested that a desire to escape the emotional demands of the relationship was one of Byron's motives for going to Greece). She visited England in 1832 and later remarried and settled in Paris. Her *Lord Byron Jugé par les Témoins de sa Vie* was published in Paris in 1868 and an English translation appeared in the same year. See Iris Origo, *The Last Attachment* (1949).

Hanson, John (died 1841), attorney with offices in Chancery Lane, London. He acted as business agent for Byron from the time he inherited the title, and was more notable for his loyalty than for his efficiency. Byron wrote numerous letters to him, and was on friendly terms with Hanson's family. The letters relating to the sale of Newstead and the legal preparations for Byron's marriage show an increasing exasperation at his slowness in conducting business. Hanson became one of Byron's executors.

Hay, Captain John. Byron had known him in England (there is a record of a wager between them at Brighton in 1808), and they met again when Hay arrived in Pisa in January 1822.

Hobhouse, John Cam (1786–1869), later (1851) Lord Broughton, politician and memoirist, and a close friend of Byron, whose executor he became. He met Byron at Cambridge in 1807 and (in the words of his *Recollections*) 'having taken my degree, I travelled with him across Portugal and Spain to Gibraltar and Malta, and thence to Albania, Greece, and Constantinople' (the tour began on 2 July 1809). He was best man at Byron's wedding, and saw him off when he left England in 1816. Soon afterwards, he joined Byron in Switzerland, and travelled with him in Italy. Himself the son of a Whig MP, Hobhouse became a Radical MP for Westminster in 1820. After Byron's death he was involved in the destruction of the memoirs. He published recollections of their travels in Europe and Asia Minor soon after the event; his account of the separation, and of the destruction of the memoirs, and his lengthy recollections, appeared posthumously (for details of all these, see the Select Bibliography).

Hodgson, Francis (1781–1852) met Byron at Cambridge in 1807, when Byron was an undergraduate at Trinity College and Hodgson an assistant tutor at King's College. His translation of Juvenal (1807) was, like Byron's *English Bards and Scotch Reviewers*, attacked by the *Edinburgh Review*. As Marchand says, 'this friendship was one of Byron's strangest. Hodgson's moral earnestness and sometimes humourless conventionality were at complete odds with Byron's sceptical proclivities'. Hodgson took orders in 1812; unsurprisingly, his attempts to turn Byron into a believer met with no success. Byron's friendship took the practical form of helping Hodgson to pay his debts and thus to marry, and it lasted until Byron went abroad in 1816. There are references to Byron in the *Memoir of the Rev. Francis Hodgson, BD* (1878).

Hone, William (1780–1842), author and bookseller, prosecuted for his *Political Litany* (1817).

Hoppner, Richard (1786–1872), British consul in Venice from 1814; he and his Swiss wife met Byron there in 1817 and became friends. Hoppner also assisted Byron with his business affairs and they corresponded frequently. The Hoppners looked after Allegra for a time before she joined her father.

Hunt, John (1775–1848), brother of Leigh Hunt (see below), with whom he was joint partner in the well-known periodical *The Examiner*. As publisher of *The Liberal*, edited by Leigh in conjunction with Byron and Shelley, he printed *A Vision of*

Judgement in the first number, was prosecuted for libel, and was found guilty and fined. He later published the last eleven cantos of *Don Juan* and Byron's subsequent work. He and Byron corresponded but never met.

Hunt, (James Henry) Leigh (1784–1859), versatile author. In 1813 he was jailed for a libel on the Prince Regent published in the liberal weekly *The Examiner*, which Hunt and his brother John (see above) had established in 1808. Byron visited him in Cold Bath Fields Prison in May 1813 and was introduced to him by Moore; further visits followed, they corresponded, and Byron helped Hunt to publish his poem *The Story of Rimini* (1816). In 1822 Hunt and his wife and six children joined Byron and Shelley at Pisa; the plan was that they should jointly edit a new periodical, *The Liberal*, to be published in London by John Hunt, but it expired after only four issues. Hunt's presence in Italy proved troublesome to Byron. His recollections of Byron are included in two books: *Lord Byron and Some of his Contemporaries* (1828) and his *Autobiography* (1850; rev. edn, 1860). The former presents a very unfavourable portrait of Byron, but the latter retracts some of the earlier judgements and revises some of the material printed earlier so as to soften the harshness of the picture. There is a biography of Hunt by Edmund Blunden (1930); see also William H. Marshall's *Byron, Shelley, Hunt, and 'The Liberal'* (Philadelphia, 1960).

Jersey, Lady. Daughter of the Earl of Westmoreland, she married in 1804 and her husband became Earl of Jersey in the following year. A well-known society hostess, she met Byron shortly after he had achieved fame with *Childe Harold*, and they became friends. He frequented her London salon, and met Madame de Staël there.

Kinnaird, The Honourable Douglas (1788–1830), son of Baron Kinnaird; he met Byron at Cambridge, where Kinnaird, who was also attending Trinity College, was already a friend of Hobhouse. Later they met frequently in London. Kinnaird persuaded Byron to join the sub-committee of management of the Drury Lane Theatre. After Byron left England in 1816, Kinnaird gave considerable assistance with his business and literary affairs and was the recipient of numerous letters. According to Count Gamba,

Kinnaird's name was one of those mentioned by Byron on his deathbed.

Lamb, Lady Caroline (1785–1828), daughter of the Earl of Bessborough; she married in 1805 William Lamb, who later, as Lord Melbourne, became one of Queen Victoria's prime ministers. Byron met her at Holland House in 1812; after the end of their brief and tempestuous affair, her infatuation did not wane and she continued to besiege him with persistent, unwelcome and wildly indiscreet attentions. Among other exploits, she disguised herself as a page, and forged a letter in order to obtain one of his portraits. Her novel *Glenarvon* (1816) contains a character based on Byron.

Lewis, Matthew Gregory ('Monk') (1775–1818), novelist, remembered for *The Monk* (1796).

Mavrocordatos, Prince Alexander (1791–1865), Greek patriot and leader. He settled in Pisa in 1818, while in exile from Greece, and became a member of Shelley's circle (Shelley's *Hellas* is dedicated to him). When revolution broke out, he returned to Greece; and Byron joined him at Missolonghi, where Mavrocordatos was commander-in-chief and governor of western Greece, in January 1824. In a letter to Murray (25 Feb 1824), Byron describes him as 'an excellent person'.

Medwin, Thomas (1788–1869), second cousin and boyhood friend of Shelley, returned from army service in India in 1819 and joined Shelley in Pisa in October 1820. He met Byron in November 1821. His *Conversations of Lord Byron* (1824; modern edn by Ernest J. Lovell, Jr, Princeton, NJ, 1966) was based on his notes made during Byron's lifetime and was an enormous success, fifteen editions being called for between 1824 and 1842 (according to Lovell, it was to a significant extent responsible for Byron's European influence). See also Lovell's biography of Medwin (Austin, Texas, 1962).

Melbourne, Lady (1749–1818) married in 1769 Sir Matthew Lamb, who was created an Irish baron in 1770 (with the title of Lord Melbourne), an Irish viscount in 1781, and an English peer in 1815; in 1784 he was appointed gentleman of the bedchamber to the Prince of Wales. She was an aunt of Annabella Milbanke, who married Byron; and her son, William Lamb (later Lord Melbourne), married Lady Caroline Ponsonby (see Lady Caroline Lamb above). When Lady Melbourne died, Byron described her as 'the best, and kindest, and ablest female I have ever known'.

Millingen, Dr Julius (1800–78), physician, attended Byron during his last days. Millingen had been sent to Greece as Surgeon-in-Chief to the army in western Greece, and was with Byron in Cephalonia (Nov–Dec 1823) and at Missolonghi. His insistence on subjecting Byron to bleeding during his last illness may have contributed to his death. Millingen later published *Memoirs of the Affairs of Greece with Various Anecdotes of Lord Byron and an Account of his Last Illness and Death* (1831).

Moore, Thomas (1779–1852), popular and successful Irish poet, who came to London in 1799, met Byron in November 1811 at the home of Samuel Rogers. Thereafter they met frequently in London; after Byron left England in 1816, they met only once, in Italy in October 1819, when Moore recorded in his journal that Byron had 'grown fat' and was writing his memoirs. Byron gave the memoirs to Moore, who sold them to Murray; at Hobhouse's insistence, they were destroyed, and Moore was one of those present in Murray's office when they were burned on 17 May 1824. His life of Byron appeared in 1830–1, and his journal (published 1853–6) also contains material on Byron.

Murray, John (1778–1843), publisher, was the son of the John Murray who established the famous firm in 1768. John Murray II was one of the founders of the *Quarterly Review*. He published *Childe Harold* and many other works by Byron, and the firm profited from Byron's enormous popularity. Byron met Scott in Murray's Albemarle Street premises in 1815. Among Murray's other authors were Jane Austen, Crabbe and Borrow.

Noel, Lady: name later taken by Lady Judith Milbanke, Byron's mother-in-law.

Orlando, Jean. Friend of Prince Mavrocordatos (see above). Acting on behalf of the Greek government, he asked Byron for a loan of 30,000 dollars 'for the payment of the Greek fleet'; Byron agreed to give two-thirds of the sum asked for. He was in one of the mourning-coaches at Byron's funeral procession.

Oxford, Lady, married Edward Harley, Earl of Oxford and Mortimer, in 1794, and was famous for her love affairs (her children were wittily referred to as 'the Harleian miscellany'). Byron met her in 1812, and after the termination of his brief affair with Lady Caroline Lamb he spent much time in Lady Oxford's company in London and at Eywood, her country home. Their affair ended when she went abroad with her husband in 1813.

Parry, Major William, was sent out to Greece by the Greek Committee in London, and arrived in Missolonghi on 7 February 1824, only a few weeks before Byron's death. During this period he lived in the same house as Byron, became a congenial drinking-companion, and saw him constantly. Byron described him as 'a fine rough subject'; according to Trelawny, he had 'a fund of pot-house stories'. His *The Last Days of Lord Byron* (1825) gives a graphic account of the poet's final sufferings. The fact that Parry was almost illiterate led to doubts being cast on his authorship; it is now believed that he provided the material, but that the work was 'ghosted' by Thomas Hodgskin.

Polidori, Dr John William (1795–1821) was engaged by Byron as his travelling physician on 28 March 1816 and was in his party when he left England on 24 April of that year and travelled to Switzerland. Vain and quarrelsome, he was dismissed on 16 September, and returned to England the following year. His diary of Byron's travels – prompted by an offer of £500 from Murray for an account to be published in book form – provides some interesting information for the period 24 April to 30 June and also covers 16 September to 30 December 1816. The original diary was later destroyed and a bowdlerised version published in 1911, edited by William Michael Rossetti, Polidori's nephew. Polidori's *The Vampyre* (1819), the outcome of a competition to write a ghost story in the Byron–Shelley circle in June 1816, was published anonymously and widely ascribed to Byron.

Rogers, Samuel (1763–1855), banker and poet, praised by Byron in *English Bards and Scotch Reviewers*, met Byron in 1811 and they saw each other frequently during the next few years. Rogers visited Byron at Pisa in April 1822. He was well-known as a malicious gossip-monger; his somewhat snide account of his first meeting with Byron (on which occasion Byron also met Moore) is given in *Recollections of the Table Talk of Samuel Rogers* (1856).

Scott, Alexander, a bachelor of independent means, was resident in Venice and may have been introduced to Byron by Hoppner (see above). He proved a congenial companion and they rode together frequently during Byron's Venetian period. Scott also joined Byron in a swimming-contest in the Lido.

Scott, Sir Walter (1771–1832), poet and novelist. He and Byron were introduced by Murray on 7 April 1815. Though they never became close friends, each admired the other's genius, and they met on various occasions until Byron left England for good. Byron read and reread Scott's novels enthusiastically, and dedicated *Cain* to him. Scott's journal and letters include references to Byron, and he reviewed the third and fourth cantos of *Childe Harold* in the *Quarterly Review* when they appeared. Although he admired Byron as a poet, he was disturbed by the vein of morbidity and misanthropy in his work.

Shelley, Mary (née Godwin) (1797–1851), daughter of William Godwin and second wife of Percy Bysshe Shelley, left England with the latter in 1814 and married him in 1816 after his first wife had committed suicide. She met Byron in April 1816, being introduced to him by Claire Clairmont, and saw much of him during his time in Switzerland. They met again in Venice in 1818, and saw each other frequently during Byron's residence in Pisa. Although many of her references to Byron are hostile, there is evidence that she was strongly attracted to him. He was of assistance to her after Shelley's death, but later she quarrelled with him. She published several novels, including *Frankenstein* (1818) and the autobiographical *Lodore* (1835), which includes a portrait of Byron, and there are references to Byron in her journal and her letters. Among various studies of her are those by R. Glynn Grylls (1938), Muriel Spark (1951), Janet Harris (1979) and Bonnie R. Neumann (1979); see also Ernest J. Lovell, Jr, 'Byron and Mary Shelley', *Keats–Shelley Journal*, II (1953) 35–49.

Shelley, Percy Bysshe (1792–1822), poet, met Byron in Sécheron, near Geneva, on 27 May 1816, and, when Byron moved into the Villa Diodati in June, Shelley became a near neighbour, the two poets meeting frequently until Shelley's departure for England on 28 August. On 22 August 1818 Shelley arrived in Venice on a visit to Byron, and he joined Byron in Pisa when he moved there in 1821. In Pisa they met constantly until Shelley's death by drowning in July 1822. Byron was present for Shelley's cremation on the beach in the following month. He had a great regard for Shelley as a man – calling him, on one occasion, 'without exception, the *best* and least selfish man I ever knew' – but little for his poetry. For his part, Shelley admired Byron's poetic genius and declared, 'I despair of rivalling Lord Byron, and there is no other with whom it is worth contending'. Shelley's poem *Julian and Maddalo* commemorates a ride with Byron in August 1818.

Sheridan, Richard Brinsley (1751–1816), dramatist and politician, met Byron in about 1813. They dined together on various occasions, and Byron greatly relished Sheridan's wit and conversational powers.

Smith, Horace (Horatio) (1779–1849), prolific author, now chiefly remembered for his *Rejected Addresses*, a volume of parodies published in 1812 in conjunction with his brother James and enormously popular. It includes a parody of *Childe Harold*. Byron described himself (on 3 Jan 1813) as 'a great admirer' of the volume.

Staël, Madame de (1766–1817), French writer, daughter of the politician Necker, wife of the Swedish Ambassador to Paris (died 1802), and mistress of the French author Benjamin Constant, in whose *Adolphe* (admired by Byron) she is portrayed. She came to England in June 1813 and soon afterwards met Byron. They met frequently thereafter; Byron found her clever but unamiable, and in his *Detached Thoughts* he ridiculed her habit of dominating the conversation; Lady Blessington reports him as observing that 'She declaimed to you instead of conversing with you.' He visited her during his residence in Switzerland.

Stanhope, Leicester (1784–1862), son of the Earl of Harrington, was appointed an agent of the Greek Committee in London on 21 September 1823 and arrived in Cephalonia on 22 November. Early in the next month he set off for Missolonghi, and between 5 January 1824, when Byron arrived there, and 21 February, when Stanhope left for Athens, they saw a good deal of each other. Stanhope's account of their relationship is included in his *Greece in 1823 and 1824* . . . .

Stendhal, pseudonym of **Henri Beyle** (1788–1842), French novelist; he and Byron met in Italy in 1816. According to Stendhal's later account, he first saw Byron at La Scala, Milan, and was greatly struck by the beauty and expressiveness of Byron's face as he listened to the music.

Taaffe, John (?1787–1862), an Irishman who had settled in Italy in 1815, was a friend of Shelley and met Byron towards the end of 1821 in Pisa. He became a minor member of the Shelley–Byron circle during that period. Taaffe played a part in the affair of the supposed burning-alive at Lucca in December 1821 and the imbroglio over the dragoon in March 1822 (see the Chronology for details of these episodes); and Byron was instrumental in finding a publisher for Taaffe's commentary on Dante.

Trelawny, Edward (1792–1881), a colourful personality who came of an old Cornish family, arrived in Pisa on 14 January 1822 and called on Byron the next day, when Byron described him to Teresa Guiccioli as 'the personification of my Corsair'. He organised the construction of Byron's schooner, the *Bolivar*, and later accompanied Byron to Greece. He was a self-dramatising character, and his numerous accounts of Byron, written at widely different periods during his long life, are highly unreliable. Harold Nicolson described him, not unfairly, as 'a liar and a cad'. His *Recollections of the Last Days of Shelley and Byron* (1858) was reworked twenty lears later as *Records of Shelley, Byron, and the Author*; both volumes are marked by his wish to depict Shelley (whom he admired) and Byron as strongly contrasted characters, an Ariel and a Caliban. His letters also contain material on Byron. He was present at Shelley's cremation; arriving at Missolonghi a few days after Byron's death, he was able to inspect the corpse and to leave a somewhat lurid account of it, including the nature of Byron's physical defect ('contraction of the back sinews . . . that prevented his heels resting on the ground'). His allegedly autobiographical *Adventures of a Younger Son* (1831) has been shown to be a tissue of romancing. There are biographies by H. J. Massingham (1930), Margaret Armstrong (1941), R. Glynn Grylls (1950) and William St Clair (1977).

Webster, James Wedderburn (born 1789), was a boon companion of Byron's during his early years in London, and visited him at Newstead. In 1810 Webster married Lady Frances Annesley; when Byron visited them at Aston Hall in 1813, he flirted systematically with Lady Frances under her husband's nose, and she is said to have been in his mind when he wrote *The Bride of Abydos*. Webster visited Byron in Genoa in the autumn of 1822, having by this time separated from his wife.

Williams, Edward (1793–1822), a half-pay lieutenant who had seen service with Medwin in India, settled in Italy, became a friend of Shelley, and was introduced by Shelley to Byron on 5 November 1821. Edward and Jane Williams (strictly speaking, they were not married) became members of the Pisan circle of Shelley and Byron; Williams saw Byron constantly, and his journal is a useful source of information for this period. Williams was drowned with Shelley. Jane is commemorated in several of Shelley's poems.

Select Bibliography

The most important source for this chronology has been, inevitably, Byron's own letters and journals, now available to the student and reader in Leslie A. Marchand's splendid edition (1973–81) in eleven volumes plus index-volume. Despite occasional inconsistencies over dates, this is a most valuable work of reference as well as an absorbing set of books for reading or browsing. Other useful sources have included the following; in addition, numerous biographies of Byron and the members of his circle have been consulted, and many of these are referred to under the appropriate names in the section of this volume titled 'The Byron Circle'. The place of publication is London unless otherwise indicated.

Blaquière, Edward, 'The Last Days of Lord Byron', *Narrative of a Second Visit to Greece* (1825).

Blessington, Countess of, *Lady Blessington's Conversations of Lord Byron*, ed. Ernest J. Lovell, Jr (Princeton, NJ, 1969).

Broughton, Lord [J. C. Hobhouse], *Recollections of a Long Life*, vols I–III (1909).

Browne, J. H., 'Voyage from Leghorn to Cephalonia with Lord Byron, and a Narrative of a Visit, in 1823, to the Seat of War in Greece', *Blackwood's Magazine*, XXXV (Jan 1834) 56–65.

Dallas, R. C., *Recollections of the Life of Lord Byron, 1808–14* (1824).

Galt, John, *The Life of Lord Byron* (1830).

Gisborne, Maria, and Williams, Edward, *Maria Gisborne and Edward E. Williams, Shelley's Friends, their Journals and Letters*, ed. Frederick L. Jones (Norman, Okla, 1951).

Guiccioli, Teresa, *My Recollections of Lord Byron, and Those of Eye-Witnesses of his Life* (New York, 1869).

Hobhouse, John Cam, *A Journey through Albania, and Other Provinces of Turkey in Europe and Asia, to Constantinople, During the Years 1809 and 1810* (1813).

——, *Account of the Separation of Lord and Lady Byron; also of the Destruction of Lord Byron's Memoirs* (privately printed, 1870).

Hodgson, Francis, *Memoir of the Rev. Francis Hodgson, BD* (1878).

Hunt, Leigh, *Lord Byron and Some of his Contemporaries* (1828).

——, *Autobiography* (1850; rev. edn, 1860).

——, *The Correspondence of Leigh Hunt*, ed. by his eldest son (1862).

Medwin, Thomas, *Medwin's Conversations of Lord Byron*, ed. Ernest J. Lovell, Jr (Princeton, NJ, 1966).

Millingen, Julius, *Memoirs of the Affairs of Greece with Various Anecdotes of Lord Byron and an Account of his Last Illness and Death* (1831).

Moore, Thomas, *The Journal of Thomas Moore, 1818–1841*, ed. Peter Quennell (1964).

——, *The Letters of Thomas Moore*, ed. Wilfred S. Dowden (Oxford, 1964).

——, *The Journal of Thomas Moore*, ed. Wilfred S. Dowden (1985).

Polidori, John William, *The Diary of Dr John William Polidori (1816) Relating to Byron, Shelley, etc.*, ed. W. M. Rossetti (1911).

Robinson, Henry Crabb, *The Diary, Reminiscences and Correspondence of Henry Crabb Robinson*, ed. T. Sadler (1869).

Rogers, Samuel, *Recollections of the Table Talk of Samuel Rogers*, ed. M. Bishop (Lawrence, Kan., 1953).

Scott, Sir Walter, *The Letters of Sir Walter Scott*, ed. H. J. C. Grierson (1932).

——, *The Journal of Sir Walter Scott*, ed. W. E. K. Anderson (Oxford, 1972).

Shelley, Mary, *The Letters of Mary W. Shelley*, ed. Frederick L. Jones (Norman, Okla, 1944).

——, *Mary Shelley's Journal*, ed. Frederick L. Jones (Norman, Okla, 1947).

Shelley, Percy Bysshe, *The Letters of Percy Bysshe Shelley*, ed. Frederick L. Jones (Oxford, 1964).

Stephen, Leslie, article on Byron in the *Dictionary of National Biography*.

The Times (1824).

Trelawny, E. J., *Recollections of the Last Days of Shelley and Byron* (1858).

——, *Records of Shelley, Byron, and the Author* (1878).

——, *Letters of Edward John Trelawny*, ed. H. Buxton Forman (1910).

The bibliography in Ernest J. Lovell, Jr, *His Very Self and Voice: Collected Conversations of Lord Byron* (New York, 1954), contains many items of minor interest.

Index

1 BYRON'S WRITINGS

2 PEOPLE

3 TOPICS